early years
wishing well

Collected rhymes, stories, songs and information text

Festivals

LEARNING RESOURCES
CENTRE
Havering College
of Further and Higher Education

Author	**Editor**	**Designer**
Lorraine Frankish	Susan Howard	Anna Oliwa
Compilers	**Assistant Editor**	**Illustrations**
Stories, rhymes and information text compiled by Jackie Andrews	Lesley Sudlow	Jessica Stockham
	Series Designer	**Cover artwork**
Songs compiled by Peter Morrell	Anna Oliwa	Alex Ayliffe

Acknowledgement:

Qualifications and Curriculum Authority for the use of extracts from the QCA/DfEE document *Curriculum guidance for the foundation stage* © 2000 Qualifications and Curriculum Authority.

The publishers gratefully acknowledge permission to reproduce the following copyright material:

Jackie Andrews for 'Japanese Children's Day' © 2001 Jackie Andrews, previously unpublished; **Karen Andrews** for 'The Fourth of July' © 2001 Karen Andrews, previously unpublished; **Jill Atkins** for 'The pancake race' © 2001 Jill Atkins, previously unpublished; **Ann Bryant** for 'The best present' and 'Bonfire night' © 2001 Ann Bryant, both previously unpublished; **Susan Eames** for 'I made a bracelet' © 2001 Susan Eames, previously unpublished; **John Foster** for 'It's Divali tonight' and 'New Year promises' © 2001 John Foster, both previously unpublished; **Barbara Garrad** for 'Three kings came riding' © 2001 Barbara Garrad, previously unpublished; **Karen King** for 'The Easter egg race', 'The Harvest Festival' and 'Just a bit of fun' © 2001 Karen King, all previously unpublished; **Johanne Levy** for 'March of the candles' © 2001 Johanne Levy, previously unpublished; **Wes Magee** for 'The big steel band' © 2001 Wes Magee, previously unpublished; **Tony Mitton** for 'Baisakhi', 'Hamantaschen chant', 'Dear Dad', 'The Dragon Boat Festival', 'Whizz, crackle, bang!' and 'Santa Claus' © 2001 Tony Mitton, all previously unpublished; **Peter Morrell** for 'At Easter time', 'Passover', 'May Day! May Day!', 'What have you have brought?' and 'Who will be in Bethlehem?' © 2001 Peter Morrell, all previously unpublished; **Jan Pollard** for 'Chinese Moon Festival' © 2001 Jan Pollard, previously unpublished; **Geraldine Taylor** for 'Toby's apple tree' © 2001 Geraldine Taylor, previously unpublished; **Stevie Ann Wilde** for 'St George's Day', 'Ganesh-Chaturthi', 'Wesak, Buddha's birthday', 'A rainy day', 'I'm sorry', 'Dancing shoes', 'A letter to a pen pal', and 'Eid-ul-Fitr' © 2001 Stevie Ann Wilde, all previously unpublished; **Margaret Willetts** for 'Holi' © 2001 Margaret Willetts, previously unpublished; **Brenda Williams** for 'April Fool's Day' © 2001 Brenda Williams, previously unpublished; **Irene Yates** for 'Joyful voices' © 2001 Irene Yates, previously unpublished.

Every effort has been made to trace copyright holders and the publishers apologize for any omissions.

Text © 2001 Lorraine Frankish
© 2001 Scholastic Ltd

Designed using Adobe Pagemaker

Published by Scholastic Ltd, Villiers House, Clarendon Avenue, Leamington Spa, Warwickshire CV32 5PR
Visit our website at www.scholastic.co.uk

1 2 3 4 5 6 7 8 9 0   1 2 3 4 5 6 7 8 9 0

British Library Cataloguing-in-Publication Data A catalogue record for this book is available from the British Library.

ISBN 0-439-01726-2

The right of Lorraine Frankish to be identified as the author of this work has been asserted by her in accordance with the Copyright, Designs and Patents Act 1988.

Contents

Early years wishing well: **Festivals**

Contents

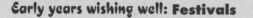

Early years wishing well: Festivals

Wishing Well: Festivals

Most children enjoy parties and special occasions, no matter how young they are. Through the poems, stories and activities that are offered in this book, they can gain firsthand experience that will allow them to build on their previous knowledge in all areas of the curriculum.

Early Years Wishing Well 'Festivals' aims to promote an awareness of the many multicultural celebrations that take place throughout the year, and it also introduces a selection of familiar events alongside some lesser-known festivals. It is designed to recognize the rich and varied cultures that exist in our society today, and covers both religious and secular events.

The majority of the festivals focus on ancient stories and legends. As these have been told and retold over hundreds of years, they have evolved in many different ways, although the main elements remain the same.

Young children may not immediately comprehend the complex ideas and beliefs that underlie many festivals. They will, however, enjoy the ideas and activities presented in this book. These are designed to capture children's interest at a level that they can appreciate. It is intended that from this early start, children will become aware of the deeper significance behind the customs and go on to understand them.

A brief explanation for each festival is given, but you may wish to undertake some further reading for your own satisfaction.

Using themes

Each story, rhyme, song and piece of information text acts as a springboard for the accompanying page of activities. Templates and photocopiable pages are also provided to support a number of these activities.

Some of the festivals will need to be approached sensitively, taking into account the children's individual family circumstances, faiths and beliefs.

All of the activities are closely linked to the requirements of the Early Learning Goals and are divided up into the six areas of learning.

As young children learn holistically, most of the ideas can be used across the curriculum and can be extended or adapted to suit their needs and abilities. The resources that are recommended can be found in most early years settings or can be easily obtained at reasonable cost.

The activities in this book have been planned to encourage children's imagination, their creativity, and their social, as well as intellectual, development. The emphasis is on learning through play: the process of the activity being of greater importance than any end product.

Holi

Today we dress in red and blue
Yellow and green, purple too.

We visit the temple, we pray together,
For Spring and Harvest and real good weather.

It's the time of Holi, no one is sad.
We sing, we dance, we trick my Dad.

We spray coloured water over each other,
Children and grown-ups, especially my brother!

After the fun we all get dry,
The flames on the bonfire roar into the sky.

We meet our friends, eat our sweets,
Enjoy the singing in the streets.

I really don't want to go to bed
But I think I must... just... rest...
my... head.

© Margaret Willetts

Holi

The Hindu festival of Holi is normally celebrated in February or March. It marks the coming of spring and the grain harvest. On the first day, a bonfire is lit and on the second day, people play practical jokes and spray each other with coloured water.

Personal, social and emotional development

★ Look at the clothes that the children are wearing. Can they find any of the colours from the poem? Discuss clothes for special occasions and talk about favourite outfits.
★ Tell the children the story of how a mischievous god called Krishna stole the clothes of milkmaids while they were bathing. Invite the children to sit in a group, facing one way, and place a scarf behind them. Ask them to listen carefully while someone tries to creep up without being heard and retrieve the scarf.

Communication, language and literacy

★ Act out the poem using props.
★ Use the photocopiable sheet on page 82 to trace over the outline of the Hindu and English words for 'Happy Holi'.

Mathematical development

★ Explore shape and space by building a 'bonfire', stacking twigs and paper.
★ Experiment with a variety of water sprayers outdoors. Measure and compare distances reached with the water.

Knowledge and understanding of the world

★ Carry out wet and dry experiments. Collect clothes of a similar thickness and spray water on them. Leave the clothes to dry in various places – inside, outside, near a radiator and so on. Which dry the quickest?
★ Fold strips of paper to make a zigzag book. Invite the children to draw pictures of Holi celebrations on each page.

Physical development

★ Encourage the children to cut thin strips of coloured paper to make pretend coloured water. Give each child a tub to collect the cuttings and let them trick a friend by throwing their coloured 'water' at them.
★ As a group, hold a large sheet of fabric (or parachute). Place small pieces of coloured paper on the sheet. Play some lively music (such as *Rangoli* by Sajan and Nitash Oderdra, from Leicester PLA, tel: 0116-2839449) and let the children shake the coloured paper up in the air so that it rains down.

Creative development

★ Make a collage of the Holi bonfire. Use dark blue or black card to represent the night sky and stick on scraps of orange, red and yellow paper to represent flames.
★ Mix red, yellow and orange powder paints, explaining that these are the colours made from natural dyes originally used at Holi. Let the children create a special picture for Holi.

Early years wishing well: Festivals

April Fool's Day

(Action rhyme)

Look... Look...
There's a sausage in your hair!
Where? Where?
April Fool!

(*Point to a child.*
Point to your own hair.
Pull at your hair.
Point to the children and smile.)

Look... stare....
There's a **Big Black Bear!**
Where? Where?
April Fool!

(*Point to a child. Stare.*
Make fingers into claws and claw
the air in front.
Jump up and look behind you.
Point to the children and smile.)

Look... there...
A rabbit eating pears
Where? Where?
April Fool!

(*Point to a child. Then point*
behind them.
Put a hand up to head like long
ears then mime eating a pear.
Put hand above eyes and look
around.
Point to the children and smile.)

Look... Look...
I have sweets I can share
Where? Where?
April Fool!

(*Point to a child.*
Mime taking sweets from your
pocket and opening a packet.
Clap hands together and then
open wide.
Point to the children and smile.)

Look... there...
A frog upon your chair!
Where? Where?
April Fool!

(*Point to a child. Then point*
behind them.
Squat like a frog.
Jump up and look behind you.
Point to the children and smile.)

© Brenda Williams

April Fool's Day

April Fool's Day is on 1 April. It is thought that the origins of this festival are linked to the beginning of spring when people were cheerful about the arrival of warmer weather and better light.

Personal, social and emotional development

★ Talk about times when the children are silly and when they are serious. Encourage them to make silly and serious facial expressions.

★ In pairs, challenge one child to make the other laugh by doing something funny.

Communication, language and literacy

★ Read nonsense rhymes, such as *Cat in the Hat* by Dr Seuss (Collins). Make up nonsense sentences such as, 'It was raining cats and dogs so I needed my toaster'.

★ Surprise the children at registration by reciting their names backwards or speaking in a high/low or loud/quiet voice. Try some jokes, for example, 'Your shoelace is undone – April Fool!'

★ Read the poem together and do the actions. Encourage the children to suggest ideas for more verses.

Mathematical development

★ Collect some plastic frogs. Sort them into size, specifying which are larger, smaller and so on. Put the frogs into colour sets and count how many of each.

★ Sing 'Ten Fat Sausages Sizzling in a Pan' from *This Little Puffin...* compiled by Elizabeth Matterson (Puffin), but change the words to 'Ten Fat Sausages Sitting in Your Hair'.

Knowledge and understanding of the world

★ Develop an understanding of forces by holding a paper frog race. Give each child a copy of the photocopiable sheet on page 83 to colour in and cut out. Place the frogs in a line and flap with a rolled-up newspaper to make them move. Shout out jokes such as, 'Hurry up, cat coming... April Fool!'.

★ Make body sound effects as you act out the poem, for example, thump chests and bang feet to show that the bears have arrived. Invite the children to make up verses with other sounds.

Physical development

★ As a group, read *We're Going on a Bear Hunt* by Michael Rosen (Walker Books) and then set off on a bear hunt around a large space. Occasionally, fool the children by 'spotting' a bear and other wild creatures.

★ Encourage the children to squat like frogs and leap across an area of floor.

Creative development

★ Make funny masks for the children to wear to surprise their parents and carers. Paint paper plates, then stick on woollen hair and paper features. Attach lolly sticks for handles.

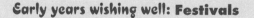

Baisakhi

Baisakhi, Baisakhi,
three days long,
(hold up three fingers)
a party for harvest
with feasting and song.
(wave hands from side to side)

We'll dance to the banghra
with tingling feet
(lift feet one by one in dance)
and all our new people
will sip the amrit.
(sip delicately from imaginary vessel)

With music and hymns
hear our festival ring,
(put up hand to ear)
as we honour our Guru,
the great Gobind Singh.
(give appropriate Sikh gesture of reverence)

Note: If a very simple version is required, the last verse can be left out.

© Tony Mitton

Baisakhi

Baisakhi marks the Sikh new year on 13 or 14 April and celebrates the founding of the Khalsa (Sikh community) by Guru Gobind Singh in 1699. The Sikh flag is lowered and the flag-pole ceremonially cleaned and covered. A procession is held with five men wearing saffron-coloured robes and turbans, and carrying swords. In the Amrit ceremony, sugared water is taken and sprinkled on those who join the Khalsa.

Personal, social and emotional development

★ Explain the importance of the Sikh flag telling the children how, at Baisakhi, people work together to take down the flag-pole to wash it. Place a small pole (broom handle or dowelling) on the floor and ask one child to pick it up alone. Try again with the help of a friend. Is it easier?

★ Discuss belonging to a community, and talk about neighbours and friends.

Communication, language and literacy

★ The Bhangra dance tells the story of a farmer's life. Act out the story. Suggest carrying the tools to the fields such as digging, looking up to the sky for rain, holding arms outstretched to feel for raindrops, wiggling fingers and moving around as the rain comes and bending over and cutting the crop. Encourage the children to add more actions.

★ Talk about the festival lasting for three days. Keep a diary for three days of all the things that you do in your group. At the end of this time, read through the diary together.

Mathematical development

★ Provide squares of paper and invite the children to fold them in half and then cut to make two triangles. Paint the triangles yellow to represent the Sikh flag and hang the flags up during Baisakhi.

Knowledge and understanding of the world

★ Show the children how to use a pulley to move a flag up and down a pole.

★ Discuss the colour of saffron and look at different shades of yellow on paint cards. Invite the children to look for similar yellows on their clothes and in their surroundings.

Physical development

★ Ask the children to sit in a circle with bare feet. Can they make their feet dance? Encourage them to wiggle their toes, move them from side to side, lift their feet one by one, and then backwards and forwards. Repeat a similar routine standing up.

Creative development

★ Talk about the costumes of the Bhangra dancers. Let the children glue scraps of green, red and yellow paper and gold foil onto white A4 card to make a Baisakhi collage.

Early years wishing well: Festivals

Hamantaschen chant

(Purim)

When you hear old Haman's name
(cup hand to ear in listening gesture)
do this, this, this.
(shake rattles in time to rhythm here, or mime)

When you hear old Haman's name
(cup hand to ear again)
stamp, boo, hiss.
(do this in rhythm, or some act it out in time to the words)

Turn him into hamantaschen,
(draw triangle in the air to show hamantaschen)
bake him in the heat.
(mime putting tray into oven with upward palm sliding forward)

Take him out and cool him off,
(slide out hand and blow to cool)
then bite, chew, eat!
(show eager eating in mime)

> Note: It may be easier for some children to chant the words while others act out the gestures and provide sound effects.

© Tony Mitton

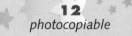

Hamantaschen chant

Purim is a Jewish festival celebrating the time when Queen Esther saved the Jewish people in the 5th century Persian empire from being slaughtered by the King's evil adviser, Haman. To celebrate the festival, the story is retold and people make loud noises and stamp their feet whenever they hear Haman's name.

Personal, social and emotional development

★ Briefly tell the story of Purim and develop the children's concentration by asking them to respond with a loud clap every time Haman's name is mentioned.

★ Read the chant several times, adding the actions to help the children to memorize the words. Repeat over several days to develop the children's long-term memories.

Communication, language and literacy

★ Encourage the children to chant the poem. Extend by inviting the children to chant their name in turn.

★ Make a sound table with drums, cymbals, tins, a basket, cardboard box and beaters. Put paper under each item and ask the children to write their name or make a mark on one of the sheets of paper to show which instrument they think makes the loudest sound.

Mathematical development

★ Queen Esther ate legumes as her kosher food (food which is considered pure to eat by

people of the Jewish faith). Select a variety of coloured beans such as red kidney, haricot and split pea. Encourage the children to count and sort them to make patterns.

Knowledge and understanding of the world

★ Invite the children to cup their hand to their ear as you talk to them. Does it help them to hear better? Make ear trumpets by rolling a 30cm semicircle of paper into a cone. Fasten with sticky tape and cut a hole in the pointed end. Use them to listen to someone talking at different levels on the other side of the room.

★ Write the name 'Haman' in chalk on a board. Provide a selection of wipes, both wet and dry, cloth and sponge, and encourage the children to try to rub it out. Which is the most effective for removing the chalk?

Physical development

★ In an open space, invite the children to move about, stamping their feet and shouting to obliterate Haman's name.

★ Explain that Purim is a time for having fun. Hold a 'parade' and play lively music as the children march or dance around the room.

Creative development

★ Make noisemakers using cardboard tubes filled with rice or dried beans. Seal the ends with masking tape and decorate with crêpe paper. Make a noise every time Haman's name is mentioned!

Joyful voices

(Saint David's Day)

Jenni really liked to listen to her teacher, Mrs Evans. She had a lovely sing-songy voice – different from the way everyone else talked.

When Jenni asked Mrs Evans about it, her teacher laughed. 'It's because I come from Wales,' she said. 'Welsh people all speak like I do.'

She showed Jenni where Wales was on the map, but it was difficult to tell how far it was in a picture. Some of the class knew. They had been to Wales on holiday.

'Let's sit on the mat and talk about it,' said Mrs Evans.

'Ye-e-es!' they all cried, and they scrambled into places on the floor.

Amy put her hand up. '*We* went to the seaside in Wales,' she said.

'*We* stayed in a caravan!' said Joshua. 'And I had a ride on a pony.'

'*We* climbed a mountain!' said Nicky.

The next day, Mrs Evans brought in pictures, postcards and old family photos to show the class. She told them all about the place she came from and what it was like growing up in the Welsh valleys.

Then she told them about Saint David, the saint who looked after Wales. He was a very good, holy man who had spent his life in the way Jesus taught, doing good things for everyone he met.

'Tomorrow is March the first,' said Mrs Evans. 'Saint David's special day. We could

have our own celebration, if you like – just the way we do in Wales.'

'Ye-e-es!' they all shouted.

Mrs Evans told them all just what they needed to bring.

It was a bright, sunny morning. Jenni and the rest of the children came to class wearing something green or yellow. Jenni had a yellow hair ribbon and Joshua wore green socks!

Mrs Evans gave each of them a daffodil she had picked from her garden, to tape to their jumpers.

Then she showed them how to make Welsh cakes. These were flat and round, with currants in them, and cooked in a flat griddle pan instead of inside the oven. When the cakes were cool, the children sprinkled them with sugar. They tasted delicious!

Finally, Mrs Evans taught them a song about the land of Wales, all in Welsh. She told them what the words meant, and said that they must sing it loudly and joyfully. Their singing would rise all the way up to heaven: Saint David would hear it and it would remind him of his old home.

Such lovely singing came from Jenni's classroom that morning, that people passing by stopped to listen – and smile!

© Irene Yates

Joyful voices

The patron saint of Wales is Dewi or David, whose feast day is celebrated on 1 March. He set up many Christian churches and monasteries and made a pilgrimage to Jerusalem. The Welsh national emblems are daffodils and leeks.

Personal, social and emotional development

★ Talk about how David spent his life trying to do good things. Can the children list some good things that they do, such as help with a younger brother or sister or care for a pet?

★ Sit the children in a circle and talk about the kind of music that makes them happy. Sing together, 'If You're Happy and You Know it Clap your Hands'.

Communication, language and literacy

★ Gather postcards, books and pictures of Wales and discuss them in small groups. Give the children plain postcards and encourage them to write messages and draw pictures.

★ Sing 'Pat-a-cake, Pat-a-cake' from *This Little Puffin...* compiled by Elizabeth Matterson (Puffin), changing the words to 'Pat-a-Welsh-cake'.

Mathematical development

★ Look at the recipe for Welsh cakes on page 84. Help the children to develop an understanding of measuring for weight using standard measures. Reinforce the names of standard measures. Follow up by letting the children help to make some Welsh cakes.

★ Ask parents and carers to let their children wear either green or yellow socks on Saint David's Day. Make a chart to show which colour was the favourite.

Knowledge and understanding of the world

★ Place one bunch of daffodils in a pot with water and another in an empty pot. Observe the daffodils over a few days. What changes and differences do the children notice?

★ Look at a map of Wales. Cut a piece of card into this shape for the children to colour. Tell them about the hills, the valleys and the seaside, and invite them to represent these on the map.

Physical development

★ Let the children roll and mould clay or play dough into leeks or daffodil shapes.

★ Discuss the Welsh coal mines and encourage the children to act out the role of a coal miner by digging, chiselling and crawling.

Creative development

★ Make a green and yellow collage using coloured fabric scraps.

★ Cut a daffodil horn from an egg box and petals from card. Paint these yellow and then attach a stem and leaves cut from green card. Staple the daffodils inside cardboard flowerpots to make a 3-D wall display.

Early years wishing well: Festivals

The best present

Carly crept downstairs so her mum wouldn't wake up. She took the big pieces of paper out of the cupboard, got the Blu-Tack, stood on a chair and started to stick the papers side by side along the wall. There was a letter written on every paper and Carly had carefully coloured them all in. All together the papers spelt I LOVE MY MUM.

'Happy Mother's Day!' said Carly, giving her mum a big hug and handing her the special card she'd made.

Carly's mum loved the card, and when she went downstairs and saw the message on the wall, she hugged Carly and said it was a wonderful surprise.

After breakfast, Carly and her mum and dad went to the village fête. The first person Carly saw was Robin Griggs. She ran over to him.

'Hi,' said Robin. 'What did you get your mum for Mother's Day?'

'I stuck a message on the wall,' said Carly. It said I LOVE MY MUM.'

'That's not a proper present,' said Robin. 'I gave my mum a big box of chocolates.'

When Carly went back to her mum and dad she felt sad. Robin was right. She should have got her mum a proper present.

'I've bought five raffle tickets,' said Carly's mum. 'I don't expect we'll win though because we never do!'

Carly and her mum and dad played hoops and bowls and knocking down cans with beanbags. They watched the tug-of-war, ate hot dogs and listened to the band. At last it was time for the raffle to be drawn.

The vicar pulled ticket after ticket out of the hat and called out the numbers but none of them matched up with Carly's mum's tickets. There was one to go.

'Number 102,' called the vicar.

'That's us,' said Carly's dad. 'Unbelievable!'

'There you are,' said the vicar handing Carly's mum a lovely big box of chocolates. 'What a nice Mother's Day present.'

Robin Griggs was standing right beside Carly.

'Now your mum's getting a proper present,' he said.

'I don't need these chocolates,' said Carly's mum to the vicar. You see I've already got the best Mother's Day present I could possibly have. Why don't you draw out another number from the hat.'

Robin Griggs looked most surprised, but Carly just smiled at him. She felt the happiest she'd felt all day.

© Ann Bryant

The best present

Mothering Sunday falls on the fourth Sunday in Lent in March or April, and is a Christian event. In recent years, it has become known as Mother's Day and people celebrate it by giving cards and presents.

Personal, social and emotional development

★ Remain sensitive to individual family circumstances as you talk about mothers, or other people who care for the children. Ask the children about times when their mother or other female carer has made them feel happy.
★ Talk about helping at home and ask the children to make a special effort on Mother's Day. Suggest that they help with a simple task such as setting the table or tidying their toys.

Communication, language and literacy

★ Working with a small group of children, write the heading 'Thank you' on a large sheet of paper. Underneath this, compile a list of all the things that the children would like to say 'thank you' to their parents and carers for. Display for the children and parents and carers to see.

Mathematical development

★ Sit six soft toys on either end of a rope for a game of 'Tug of War'. Give the children a dice to throw and ask them to count the spots to determine how many places each team should move back.

★ Encourage number recognition by giving half of the children a raffle ticket and the others the same set of numbers written on cards. Can they find a pair?

Knowledge and understanding of the world

★ Make a set of skittles from empty plastic drinks bottles. Let the children fill them with different materials such as sand, water and pebbles, and experiment to see which is the easiest to knock over with a beanbag.
★ Look at the behaviour of animal mothers and babies using books such as *Where's My Kitten?* by Michele Coxon (Happy Cat Books) and *Kangaroos Have Joeys* by Philippa-Alys Browne (Barefoot Books).

Physical development

★ Talk about Carly's message to her mum. Write out a similar message in the centre of a sheet of coloured A4 paper. Give a sheet to each child and ask them to seal their message by folding the sheet in half as many times as they can. Encourage them to press down on each fold and then seal with sticky tape.

Creative development

★ Lay out rose petals to dry and watch the changes during the drying process. When completely dry, let each child place some in the centre of a circle cut from muslin, gather up the edges and tie with ribbon. Give as gifts to someone special on Mother's Day.

Early years wishing well: Festivals

Saint George's Day

There is a story from a long time ago about a dragon that lived in the mountains, near to a little town in North Africa. People were very frightened of it. They didn't want the dragon living near them, so they sent the mayor of the town to chase it away.

'Please stop frightening us – and go away,' said the mayor in his sternest voice.

The dragon just ROARED and blew the mayor's hat down the mountain. '*You* go away,' it said, 'and bring me a nice, tasty lamb for my dinner.'

The mayor ran back to the town as fast as he could. He told the people what the dragon had said, and that afternoon they sent a lamb dinner up to the dragon.

The dragon was very pleased. After that, whenever he grew hungry he ROARED for another meal. If the people in the town weren't quick enough, he flew over their houses, blowing fire and smoke at them.

So the people sent the dragon more and more food.

Until they didn't have any left.

The mayor went to see the dragon again, quaking in his boots. 'We have no more food to give you,' he said.

The dragon ROARED again, this time blowing the mayor down the mountain. 'Bring me the king's daughter!' it said.

Bruised and very worried, the mayor picked himself up and hobbled back to the town. When the people heard what the dragon wanted, they were very sad. They loved the little princess very much.

But the princess was very brave. She told them all not to worry: she was sure God would look after her, and she went by herself to meet the dragon. Just as the dragon was making its way towards the little girl, a young man arrived riding a horse and carrying a sword and a shield.

He fought the dragon and killed it, then he took the princess back to the town. The king gave him a great deal of money for saving the princess, but the young man gave it all away to the poor. He told the people to believe in God, to look after each other and not be afraid any more.

The young man's name was George. Many, many years later he was called *Saint George* because he was such a brave, kind man. Pictures of Saint George show him with a red cross on his shield, and the kings of England put this red cross of Saint George on their flag.

People remember Saint George on the 23 April every year.

© Stevie Ann Wilde

Saint George's Day

Saint George is the patron saint of England, and people celebrate Saint George's Day on 23 April. Stories of Saint George killing a dragon to save a princess were brought to England at the end of the 11th century by soldiers returning from the Crusades. Saint George's flag is a red cross on a white background.

Personal, social and emotional development

★ Ask the children to talk about times when they have been brave. Invite them to bring in a special teddy or security blanket to extend the discussion.

★ Talk about the dragon's fire, reinforcing the dangers of fire. Support the message by chanting the rhyme, 'Matches, matches, never touch. They can hurt you very much'.

Communication, language and literacy

★ Look at books and pictures of castles, such as *How Castles Were Built* by Peter Hicks (Wayland). Talk about life in a castle.

★ Using the photocopiable sheet on page 85, write the word 'dragon' spaced out across the body of the dragon. Give each child a copy, cut into six pieces and ask them to reassemble the dragon to reveal the word.

Mathematical development

★ Invite the children to build a castle from wooden blocks. Encourage them to be architects and plan the shape, working out which blocks to use and where. Consider towers, drawbridges and thick walls.

★ Cut a large rectangle from red card and four smaller rectangles from white card. Encourage the children to use the shapes to make Saint George's flag.

Knowledge and understanding of the world

★ Investigate clothes and costumes that might have been worn during Saint George's time. Talk about arms and armour.

★ Using the photocopiable sheet on page 85 cut out a dragon for each child. Ask them to colour it in. Tape it to a thin stick and shine a light on it to make a dragon-shaped shadow on the wall.

★ Discuss how the dragon blew the mayor's hat down the mountain. Move a ball, a small car, an empty box and a hat down a slide.

Physical development

★ Play a chasing game of dragon and villagers, letting each child have a turn as the dragon.

★ Celebrate 23 April by country dancing to traditional folk music.

Creative development

★ Ask parents and carers to provide their children with an old sock to make a dragon puppet. Add features by gluing on scraps of felt, and attach a bright fabric flame coming from the dragon's mouth.

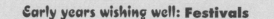

The Easter egg race

Tomorrow is Easter Day. We're having an Easter egg race with our friends. We'll all roll eggs down the path in our back garden and see which one reaches the bottom first. But first, we're going to decorate our eggs for the race and my mum shows us what to do.

The eggs have to be boiled, or they would just break and make a mess. Mum puts them in a saucepan of bubbly water on the cooker for us and we have to wait for about ten minutes so that we can be sure they are really hard. What a long time to wait!

At last the eggs are done, so Mum switches off the cooker and puts them into cold water so that they cool down quickly.

Now they are ready for decorating!

We fetch our paints and put on our aprons while Mum covers the table with newspaper. She puts a cup of water in the middle of the table for us to dip our brushes into and wet them.

'You can paint a pattern or a picture on your egg,' she says.

We put each egg in an eggcup to hold it steady, and paint one half of our eggs first. When it's dry we turn it over and paint the other half.

I paint a funny face on my egg. Janine covers hers with blue and yellow stars, and Josh paints his with black and white stripes for his favourite football team. My brother George paints his egg all red, then he paints yellow squiggly snakes all over it.

Now it's time for the race. We take our painted eggs outside and kneel at the top of the path. Mum says, 'Ready, steady, GO!' and we send our eggs rolling and bumping down the path while we run behind, laughing and shouting at them to go faster! Over and over they roll. Down and down the steps they bounce.

Whose egg will get to the bottom of the path first?

Look – it's the egg with a funny face! It's mine! 'I've won!' I shout.

Janine's egg comes second, and we all tease Josh about his team being rubbish anyway.

Mum hands out the Easter egg prizes. But where is George's egg? Our dog, Candy, has run off with it and buried it in her basket! But Mum gives him a prize for the egg that came in last, so we're all winners – even Candy.

© Karen King

The Easter egg race

The Easter egg is a symbol of new life. In many places throughout the world, there are egg-rolling events and egg hunts. The date of Easter varies between March and April.

Personal, social and emotional development

★ Give a small group of children a real egg to examine, explaining that they must handle it with care as it is fragile and could break.

★ Talk about how the children in the story helped to set up the painting activity. Ask the children to prepare an activity. Let them cover the table with newspaper and set out aprons, paints and brushes. Allow them to help with tidying up afterwards.

Communication, language and literacy

★ Draw two lines across a sheet of A4 paper to represent a winding path. Help to develop pencil control by inviting the children to draw a similar path underneath.

★ Ask the children to retell the story with their own pictures. Add a few lines of text underneath each illustration and give more able children an opportunity to copy this.

Mathematical development

★ Paint a pattern of coloured stripes for the children to copy onto a piece of oval-shaped paper, to represent a patterned Easter egg.

★ Compare, sort and count a selection of eggs in various sizes and shades. Extend the activity by providing a wider variety of eggs such as duck, quail and goose.

Knowledge and understanding of the world

★ Crack an egg onto a saucer and examine it. Poach or fry the egg and examine it again. What changes have taken place?

★ Investigate the life cycle of chickens and ducks through books, posters and puzzles, for example, *Life Cycle of a Chicken* by Angela Royston (Heinemann) and *Daisy and the Egg* by Jane Simmons (Orchard Books).

★ Roll a variety of balls down a slope.

Physical development

★ Practise rolling movements. Can the children roll across a room? Try rolling down a slight incline outside. (**NB** Ensure that the area is free from dangerous objects.)

★ Set up an egg hunt. Hide small oval cards around your setting, making some easier to find than others. When the children have found a card, encourage them to put it into a basket. When all the cards have been found, exchange them for little chocolate eggs, sharing them among the children.

Creative development

★ Design a badge as a reward for taking part in an egg race. Cut small pieces of card into oval shapes for the children to decorate. Attach double-sided tape so that they will stick to the children's clothes.

Japanese Children's Day

My name is Taro Yamaguchi (*Ta-ro Yam-uh-goo-chee*) and I live in Tokyo, in Japan. I am very excited because today is the fifth of May, when we have a holiday to celebrate Children's Day. We have already decorated the house with leaves from iris plants, to keep it safe from bad things!

My father, mother and grandmother are going to take my little sister Yukari (*Yuh-ka-ree*) and me to the park for a picnic.

This day is also known as Boy's Day. That's because long ago, families used to give thanks on this day for having a boy in the family and hoped he would grow up to be healthy and strong. But today we celebrate *all* children – and their mothers who have taken care of them – and wish them good and happy lives!

It is not far to the park. I help carry the baskets and Yukari rides in the baby buggy. We find a good place by the river in between other happy families, and put out the rugs to sit on and the folding chairs for Mother and Grandmother.

Father shows Yukari and me how to make paper boats and we float them on the river, watching them sail away as the water flows past.

Soon it is time to eat. I wonder if Mother has remembered the special rice cakes... yes, there they are! All wrapped up in oak leaves to make them taste good. Yukari and I eat two or three each – but we mustn't eat too many. Tonight we will have a big family meal together in our apartment, with my Aunt and Uncle and two cousins.

Children's Day is a good day. I wish it happened *every* day!

© Jackie Andrews

Japanese Children's Day

Japanese Children's Day, also known as Kodomono-hi, is on 5 May. Families with young children fly colourful streamers and kites shaped like carp fish. The carp is a symbol of strength and determination.

Personal, social and emotional development

★ Discuss how Taro helped to carry the baskets. Invite the children to carry some toys when it is time to tidy up.

★ Explain that carp can swim upstream. To do this, they must swim against the current, so they have a lot of determination. Demonstrate the force of water by letting the children place their hands under fast-running water from a tap, then challenge them to try something which takes practice and determination, such as learning to hop on one leg.

Communication, language and literacy

★ Give each child a copy of the photocopiable sheet on page 86. Develop emergent writing by encouraging them to draw rows of scales using colourful pens. More able children could write some simple facts about the festival.

★ Act out a visit to the park for a special picnic. Discuss what you need and draw up a list of items such as a rug, chairs and a ball. Spend time 'packing' the items and decide who will carry what. Stop to cross roads, to look at animals or visit the shops.

Mathematical development

★ Set out six plates of a teaset and ask the children to gather dolls and soft toys for a special picnic. Count the plates together. How many toys can attend the picnic? If the children have brought more than six dolls, count together how many remain. Extend by playing 'Hide-and-seek' with the toys, encouraging the children to add and subtract.

Knowledge and understanding of the world

★ Visit a local park and on your return, map out the route taken on a large sheet of paper. Encourage the children to draw in things that they noticed on the journey.

★ Put a bunch of irises on display and let the children touch, smell and look at them. Discuss the colour and then send the children on a colour hunt to find purple items such as clothing, displays, books and toys.

Physical development

★ Tell the children that they need to keep active in order to remain strong and healthy. Try some exercises together, such as stretching up high, bending over and touching toes, jumping and running.

Creative development

★ Go outside to gather a few grasses and daisies. Ask the children to create a picture of the picnic in the story. Provide A4 card, PVA glue, spreaders and scraps of coloured paper.

Early years wishing well: Festivals

Passover

(Tune: 'Bobby Shaftoe')
Bible reference: Exodus 12:1–30

| F | | | C | | |

1. Pass - o - ver what does it mean?__ Pass - o - ver what does it mean?__

| F | | | B♭ | C7 | F |

Pass - o - ver what does it mean?__ Tell us all a - bout it.

2. Passover is all about
Passover is all about
Passover is all about
Moses and the Israelites.

3. God said, 'Moses take your friends,'
God said, 'Moses take your friends,'
God said, 'Moses take your friends,'
'Away from horrid Pharaoh.'

4. 'You've been cruel,' God said to Pharaoh,
'You've been cruel,' God said to Pharaoh,
'You've been cruel,' God said to Pharaoh,
'Now you will be punished.'

5. 'I will send a deadly plague
I will send a deadly plague
I will send a deadly plague
On all Egyptian houses.'

6. 'Israelites paint your door frames red
Israelites paint your door frames red
Israelites paint your door frames red
I'll know who to pass over.'

7. Passover's to celebrate
Passover's to celebrate
Passover's to celebrate
When God saved all His people.

© Peter Morrell

Passover

Passover (Pesach) is celebrated in March or April. It is an important dates in Jewish religion and remembers the Israelites' escape from slavery in Egypt. They daubed their doorposts with lamb's blood so that the Angel of Death would pass over their home.

Personal, social and emotional development

★ Raise the children's awareness of being tolerant towards others. Let them cut out pictures of people from magazines. Ensure that your collection includes pictures of those with disabilities, old and young and ethnic minorities. Glue the pictures together on a large sheet of paper and add a caption such as 'Everyone different, everyone welcome'.
★ Involve the children in preparations for Passover by washing tables and chairs.

Communication, language and literacy

★ Invite the adults in your setting to act out the story of Passover for the children to watch.
★ At supper time, Jews read and sing from a book called the 'Haggadah' (story of the Exodus). It is traditional for the youngest children to ask questions at this time. Sing the Passover song and then encourage the children to ask questions about its meaning.

Mathematical development

★ Jews eat matzo – unleavened bread – during Passover. This bread is cooked for no longer than 18 minutes, so it does not have a chance to rise. To understand the passage of time, show the children a timer set for 18 minutes. When the timer sounds, gather together and list all the things that you have done during 18 minutes.

Knowledge and understanding of the world

★ Invite a parent or local resident from a Jewish family to visit and talk about Passover.
★ During the Passover supper, people drink four glasses of wine or grape juice. Let the children taste a variety of grape juices including red, white and sparkling.

Physical development

★ Removing every bit of hametz (cereal products containing yeast) is an important part of the Passover preparations. Practise bending and stretching while doing exaggerated actions of sweeping, scrubbing and rubbing.
★ A game of searching for hametz is a fun part of Passover. Hide pieces of bread for the children to find.

Creative development

★ Cut a 'door' into a piece of A4 card. Encourage the children to carefully paint around the door with red paint to symbolize the daubing of the doorposts.
★ Create a seed collage by gluing wheat grain in patterns onto a sheet of card.

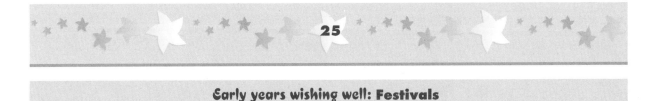

At Easter time

C   G7   *   C

1. At East-er time, at East-er time. There's lots to do at East-er time. But
2. choc-'late eggs
3. new-born lambs

F   G7   C F C

East-er time is all a-bout the time when Je-sus died and came a-live a-gain.

Ask the children what else happens/they do at Easter time.

© Peter Morrell

At Easter time

Easter, one of the most important dates in the Christian calendar, celebrates the resurrection of Christ from death on the cross. It occurs around March or April and the seasonal change from cold to warm, with its effect on plants and animals, adds to the festival's message of hope and rejuvenation.

Personal, social and emotional development

★ Talk about how people wear decorated bonnets at Easter. Invite the children to wear a favourite hat as you hold an Easter parade.

★ Use books such as *I am a Duck* by Linda Bygrave (David Bennett Books) or *The Very Hungry Caterpillar* by Eric Carle (Hamish Hamilton) to look at animal life cycles.

Communication, language and literacy

★ Go on a walk and look for signs of spring such as catkins, lambs and ladybirds. In the town, look for Easter eggs in shops and church notices for Easter.

★ Invite parents and carers to join a special singing session. Sing 'At Easter time' and other songs that the children enjoy. *This Little Puffin...* compiled by Elizabeth Matterson (Puffin) has a good collection of songs.

Mathematical development

★ Investigate hot cross buns, noticing the shape of the bun and the cross. How many pieces will there be when the bun is cut in half? Into quarters? Talk about the shape of the cut pieces.

★ Look at the shape of the cross and ask the children to find other cross shapes, for example on flags, road signs and first-aid kits.

Knowledge and understanding of the world

★ Lambs are a favourite symbol at Easter. Investigate balls of wall and woollen clothes. Help the children to make comparisons between manufactured and natural fabrics.

★ Let the children examine an old discarded bird's nest and attempt to build a similar one. Gather twigs, leaves and moss and stick into a clay or play dough base.

Physical development

★ Invite the children to be Easter bunnies, and ask them to crouch down and hop around.

★ Set up an egg and spoon race outside. Give each child a hard-boiled egg and a wooden or plastic spoon. Can they balance the egg on the spoon as they run to the finishing line?

Creative development

★ Make a mobile for an Easter tree. Copy the photocopiable sheet on page 87 onto card and cut out the shapes. Provide collage materials including shredded paper and let the children decorate the shapes. Attach thread then suspend the mobiles on a branch secured in a pot or box.

May Day! May Day!

(Tune: 'Baa, Baa, Black Sheep')

May Day! May Day! Flow-ers in the spring. May Day! May Day! Dance and sing.

Dance round the may-pole and weave in and out, Make stream-er pat-terns on this round-a-bout.

May Day! May Day! Flow-ers in the spring. May Day! May Day! Dance and sing.

© Peter Morrell

Early years wishing well: Festivals

May Day! May Day!

May Day celebrates the end of winter and the start of new life. Dancing around the maypole and morris dancers with their tapping sticks and jingling bells are a traditional part of the celebrations.

Personal, social and emotional development

★ Tell parents and carers that you will be celebrating May Day. Ask them to let their children wear something special for the occasion. Encourage the children to talk to the group about their outfits.

★ Ask the children to bring in a few flowers or leaves for the festival (garden flowers or weeds will do). Let each child talk about their flowers and then display them, allowing everyone to touch, smell and examine them.

Communication, language and literacy

★ Arrange a visit from a keen gardener. Ask them to bring some of the tools that they use, flowers that they have grown or photographs of their garden. Invite them to talk about how the garden changes throughout the year.

★ Examine a fresh flower. Use the photocopiable sheet on page 88 to reinforce the names of the different parts of the flower.

Mathematical development

★ Grow some cress from seed. Place blotting paper in a plastic tray and sprinkle on the seeds. Let the children water the seeds and watch them grow. Discuss how long this takes and measure how much the seeds grow.

★ Buy two packets each of several varieties of seeds and then discuss them together. Mix the packets up and ask the children to find pairs. For more able children, place the packets face down.

Knowledge and understanding of the world

★ Take a walk outdoors and encourage the children to look upwards at flowering trees. Common trees such as hawthorn, elder and horse chestnut are all in blossom in May.

Physical development

★ Attach two-metre lengths of crêpe-paper streamers to a post or hat stand. Ask the children to hold a streamer as they dance around the 'maypole'. **NB** Make sure that the post is secure.

★ Let the children choose bells or rhythm sticks to play as they dance and sing 'May Day! May Day!'.

Creative development

★ Make a floral decoration to wear. Give each child a fresh flower such as a carnation, a sprig of small leaves (fern or privet), cotton wool and silver foil. Place the leaves and flower together. Dampen the cotton wool and wrap it around the stalks. Wrap them securely in foil then attach to the children's clothes with a safety pin.

Wesak, Buddha's birthday

On Wesak day we meet our friends
To celebrate this day.
We are kind to everything that lives,
This is the Buddha's way.

Walking, walking round and round
People come to think and pray,
Three times round the holy tower
To remember Buddha's birthday.

We think about Buddha and whisper his name,
And think of the things he would say.
Next we remember the holy men
Who teach us to follow his way.

We light the lamps and bring the flowers
And send the Wesak cards today.
We listen to stories and sing our songs
To celebrate Buddha's birthday.

© Stevie Ann Wilde

Early years wishing well: Festivals

Wesak, Buddha's birthday

Wesak marks the birth, enlightenment and death of Buddha. It is held when there is a full moon, usually in May or June. Buddhists gather in temples to release captured birds and to offer prayers. It is a time to remember Buddha's teaching about kindness. A part of the celebrations include pouring perfumed water over the image of Buddha.

Personal, social and emotional development

★ Develop listening skills by whispering the children's names and encouraging individuals to respond when they hear their name.
★ Talk about being kind to everything that lives, and give the children examples of how they can do this. For example, ask them to feed the wild birds with bird food, or free an insect that is trapped indoors.

Communication, language and literacy

★ Gather together some items associated with Wesak such as oil lamps, flowers, incense sticks and food. Label each item and let the children handle them and talk about them. Extend the activity by asking the children to draw a picture and 'write' about it.

Mathematical development

★ Talk about Buddha's birthday and the children's birthdays. Make a chart using twelve pieces of A4 card, with the name of one month on each. List the children's birthdays on the appropriate card, then discuss which month has the most birthdays.

Knowledge and understanding of the world

★ Discuss different forms of light such as candles, torches and electrical lights. Test some torches to see which is the brightest by shining them on the ceiling. Look inside a torch to see where the batteries and bulb fit.
★ Let the children make a variety of perfumed waters. Try infusing rose petals with warm water or make, and then cool, different varieties of herb tea for the children to smell.

Physical development

★ Give the children some bells to jingle and invite them to dance and move about a large open area as you recite the poem.
★ In a safe place, burn some incense. Invite the children to walk around the room quietly and slowly, as the monks sometimes do when they contemplate and pray.

Creative development

★ Give each child a copy of the photocopiable sheet on page 89. Encourage them to decorate and then cut out the outline. Show them how to fold a piece of A4 paper into a fan shape to represent wings. Cut a slit in each bird's body, then push the wings through. Attach thread to the birds and hang up near a window.

Dear Dad

(Father's Day poem)

Dear Dad, I wrote
these words for you,
to put upon
the card I drew.

I did my best,
tried really hard,
to make a clever
father's card.

The other dads,
I guess, are fine.
But, Dad, you're special
'cos you're mine.

So have a happy
Father's Day.
I'm glad that you're
my dad – hooray!

© Tony Mitton

Early years wishing well: Festivals

Dear Dad

Father's Day dates back to 1908. It began in America as a day to honour fathers or men who have helped to bring up children. It is celebrated on the third Sunday in June.

Personal, social and emotional development

★ Discuss with the children what makes their fathers special. Remain sensitive to individual family circumstances, talking about 'someone special', if appropriate.

★ Ask the children to suggest something that they can try really hard to do well. Prompt them with ideas, for example, trying to keep sand in the tray while they are playing. Praise their achievements afterwards.

Communication, language and literacy

★ Encourage the children to think about sequences as they talk about a special day. Invite them to recount their day from morning, through midday to evening. Follow this by reading *The Snowman* by Raymond Briggs (Hamish Hamilton), and talking about the sequence of events.

Mathematical development

★ Using the photocopiable sheet on page 90, cut out the shapes and challenge the children to assemble them in the shape of a tie. Once they have achieved this, let the children colour the pieces, then stick them onto a piece of paper in the correct shape.

★ Talk about size, for example, are the children's daddies bigger or smaller than they are? Extend the discussion by reading the story of 'Goldilocks and The Three Bears' (Traditional), and talking about Daddy Bear's big chair, bowl and bed.

Knowledge and understanding of the world

★ Invite the children to make a medal for a special father or person. Provide a variety of coins and show them how to make rubbings by placing a sheet of paper over a coin and rubbing with a wax crayon until an image appears. Help to cut out the rubbings, then attach to lengths of cotton to make medals.

Physical development

★ Ask the children to move around an open area, making appropriate movements when you call out a command. For example, shout, 'walk like a big daddy'. Then try a contrasting movement, for example, 'crawl like a small baby'. When the children are confident, try animal movements, for example, 'stretch like a cat' or 'plod like an elephant'.

Creative development

★ Invite the children to make a gift for their father or other special person to carry in his wallet. Cut card into credit card-size pieces and let the children decorate both sides with colourful drawings. Cover the cards with sticky-backed plastic.

The Fourth of July

(American Independence Day)

Hooray for the Fourth of July,
Hooray for the U S of A!
Hooray for seventeen seventy six –
The first Independence Day!

Hooray for the Big Parade
And the colourful marching bands.
Led by the drum majorettes –
Twirling their sticks in their hands.

Hooray for the bobbing balloons,
For the streamers that fly through the air.
For bunting and ribbons on every street:
Red white and blue everywhere!

Hooray for the waving flags,
For fireworks lighting the sky,
Hooray for the Stars and Stripes!
Hooray for the Fourth of July.

© Karen Andrews

Early years wishing well: Festivals

The Fourth of July

On 4 July 1776, America claimed its independence from England. Each year on this date, Americans celebrate with barbecues, picnics and family gatherings.

Personal, social and emotional development

★ Talk about being independent. Ask the children to think how much help a new baby needs. List some of the things that the children can do now, that they couldn't do when they were babies such as dressing themselves or washing their hands.

Communication, language and literacy

★ Write the initials USA on a piece of card and discuss with the children what the letters stand for. Write out the children's initials in large letters for them to copy. Does anyone have the same initials?
★ Find 4 July on a calendar. Tell the children that this is a special date for Americans – it is their country's birthday. Discuss when the children's birthdays are and sing 'Happy Birthday' together.

Mathematical development

★ Provide the children with red, white and blue paper triangles. Invite them to help you to make bunting by folding over the shortest edge of each triangle and taping to a long piece of string. Arrange the triangles in a repeating pattern.

Knowledge and understanding of the world

★ Can the children blow up a balloon? Show them how to use a balloon pump and discuss how the balloon gets bigger as it fills with air. Extend the activity by looking at how a bicycle pump or hairdryer uses air.
★ Give the children a selection of ribbons to examine. Discuss texture, colour, lengths and uses of the ribbons. Attach the ribbons to a wire hanger and place them outside or near a window to create a mobile.

Physical development

★ Invite the children to join the Big Parade, marching around, one behind the other, as they play musical instruments.
★ Arrange the children in a circle and ask them to pretend to be giant fireworks lighting the sky. Ask them to crouch down and then, when you clap, jump up and move around, making crackling and whizzing sounds.

Creative development

★ Let the children make streamers to fly through the air. Paint a cardboard kitchen-roll tube with bright colours. When dry, use PVA glue to attach strips of bright crêpe paper, about 30cm long, to one end.
★ Make a banner. In large letters, print the words 'Hooray for the Fourth of July' on a sheet of A1 paper. Provide the children with red, white and blue paints and small sponges and ask them to print around the letters.

Ganesh-Chaturthi

An elephant is big and strong
He moves things easily.
So Ganesha is also strong
To help my family.

We see him on his festival,
He is painted new and bright.
We put around him pretty things
Like tinsel, paper and light.

We see his face and four strong arms
With an axe and a sweet and a string.
And his hand that shows us, 'Do not fear!'
We can pray to him and sing.

When we come to the end of his festival
And this is the very last day,
He is dipped three times in the river –
Then we watch as he floats away.

© Stevie Ann Wilde

Ganesh-Chaturthi

Legend has it that Lord Shiva's son had the head of an elephant. Many Hindus believe that Ganesha can help to solve problems and remove obstacles. He is popular for bringing laughter and happiness and for his love of sweets.

Personal, social and emotional development

★ Ask the children to sit in a circle and to pass on a smile. The first child smiles at the child on the left, who turns to their left and smiles at the next child, and so on. Carry on until everyone has had a smile!

Communication, language and literacy

★ Use the photocopiable sheet on page 91 to develop writing skills. Encourage the children to use coloured pencils to join the elephants' trunks and tails together. Mount the completed sheets on the wall to make a linking elephant frieze.

★ Help the children to design their own sweet packets using paper and felt-tipped pens. Encourage them to think of a name for their sweets and to write in on their packet.

Mathematical development

★ Talk about big and little animals. Sort a variety of soft toy animals according to size. Develop the activity by telling a story. For example, tell the children that the animals have to cross a very wide river, and the smallest ones need some help. Can they find the smallest animals from the selection?

★ Sing 'One Grey Elephant Balancing' from *This Little Puffin...* compiled by Elizabeth Matterson (Puffin). Place a skipping rope on the ground and invite one more child to stand on the rope as the song progresses.

Knowledge and understanding of the world

★ Draw two wavy lines on a sheet of A3 card to represent a river. Draw and cut out a simple elephant shape and attach a paper clip to one side with sticky tape. Place the card across two piles of books then encourage the children to move the elephant down the river by moving a magnet underneath the paper.

Physical development

★ To demonstrate how an elephant uses its trunk, challenge the children to pick up a table-tennis ball by sucking through a drinking straw.

Creative development

★ Ice and decorate marshmallows. Mix icing sugar with water and encourage the children to spread this over the marshmallows. Let them add a few silver balls or jelly sweets.

★ Make a display of Ganesha's head. Cut a head, trunk and two tusks from card. Invite the children to paint the pieces and, when dry, glue them together. Add eyes and wrinkles! Decorate with gold and silver scraps and tinsel.

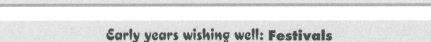

A rainy day

(Saint Swithun's Day)

'It will be your birthday soon, Ruthie,' said Ruthie's mum to her one morning. 'Would you like to have a party with your friends?'

'Oh, yes, *please*!' said Ruthie. 'And can I have a pink birthday cake?'

Mum laughed. 'If that's what you want,' she said. 'It will be a lovely way to celebrate your special day.'

The day of the party, Ruthie helped her mum make little cakes, jellies and sandwiches. Mum made a beautiful birthday cake decorated with pink icing, and put it in the centre of the table. Ruthie and her friends wore their best clothes. They had a very happy time playing games, dancing and singing 'Happy Birthday!' to Ruthie.

But when it was time for everyone to go home, it was pouring with rain.

'Oh, no!' said Ruthie's mum when she saw the weather. 'It mustn't rain today!'

'Why not?' asked Ruthie.

'Today is Saint Swithun's Day,' her mum said. 'Now it will rain for forty days!' She told Ruthie about Saint Swithun.

'A very long time ago there was a very holy man in Winchester, called Swithun. He was very kind to people, and even had a bridge built over the river so that they could easily cross from one side to the other. Swithun loved to tell everyone about God's love for them.

'One little story tells how an old lady dropped her basket of eggs and broke them. Swithun prayed, asking God to mend the eggs for her. When he picked up the basket, all the eggs were whole again!

'When Swithun died, his body was buried in the churchyard, just where he had always wanted. Later, everyone thought it would be much nicer to have a special place for him *inside* the big church. But on the 15 July, the day they moved Swithun's body into the church, there was a terrible storm. It rained and it rained. It rained for forty days.

'Now, people say that if it rains on 15 July, it will rain for forty days again. We call it Saint Swithun's day. So you and Saint Swithun share the same special day, Ruthie.'

'Is it going to rain for another forty days?' asked Ruthie.

'We'll just have to wait and see,' laughed her mum.

© Stevie Ann Wilde

Swithun lived from about 800 to 862. He was the Bishop of Winchester. His tomb was destroyed in 1538. In the Norman Cathedral, a modern monument now stands on the site of the old shrine. Winchester Cathedral is dedicated to St Paul, St Peter and St Swithun.

A rainy day

Saint Swithun was a bishop in the 9th century. His remains were moved against his wishes from a common grave to the grounds of Winchester Cathedral on 15 July and, as retribution, it is said to have rained for the following forty days. Today, the weather on Saint Swithun's Day is said to determine the weather for the next forty days.

Personal, social and emotional development

★ Encourage the children to think of outdoor activities that they could do indoors when it rains, such as an indoor picnic or a mini play. Compile the ideas into a 'A rainy day' book and design a cover, then carry out the activities on rainy days.

Communication, language and literacy

★ Record a few weather forecasts onto a cassette when rain is predicted, and play these to the children. Talk to them about the words used such as heavy, light or scattered. Encourage the children to think of their own words to describe different types of rainfall.

Mathematical development

★ Arrange two ropes measuring about two metres each on the floor, one metre apart. Tell the children that this is a bridge over a river, which they must cross. Let the children throw a dice to determine how many steps they must take to move along the 'bridge'.

★ Make a rain gauge with a tall jar and a funnel. Place this in an open space outside and collect the rainfall over a period of time. Check the bottle every day and mark each increase with a marker pen. Use a ruler to measure the total rainfall.

Knowledge and understanding of the world

★ Take the children outside after it has been raining and look at puddles. Talk about reflection and moisture. Draw around a puddle with chalk, then check it again when the weather is drier. What has happened?

Physical development

★ Play 'Mars' from Gustav Holst's *The Planets' Suite*. Ask the children to dance and move according to the music. Can they represent the storm as it brews and gets more violent, and then as it calms down?

★ Invite the children to practise their cutting skills. Give each child a large egg-shaped piece of card. Ask them to cut it into several pieces, and then let them try to reassemble the pieces to mend the egg.

Creative development

★ On a wet day, let the children take a piece of paper outside and collect a few raindrops. When they return, give them coloured markers and ask them to draw a rainy day picture. Encourage them to observe the colours changing on the damp paper.

The Dragon Boat Festival

Today was the day of the Dragon Boat Festival. I watched my father take part in the Dragon Boat Race.

First, the different teams put the tails and heads on their boats to make them look like dragons. Then they painted white dots in the eyes of the dragons, making them look fierce and alive. While this was happening, people burned sticks of incense or set off firecrackers. Bang! Bang! BANG!

Then everyone pushed paper money into the mouths of the dragons or dropped it into the river. They said that this would stop bad spirits spoiling the festival.

At the start of the race, the teams got into their dragon boats. Each boat had twenty paddlers. My father was one of them! Then there was one person to steer the boat and one person to beat the big drum.

It was all very noisy and the boats sped away very fast as soon as the race began.

My father's boat didn't win this time, but he said it didn't matter. The important thing was for everyone to take part and try hard.

My mother painted a special sign on my forehead for the festival, and pinned some little packets on my clothes. They were filled with spices and medicines, and smelled nice. Then we had our meal of special dumplings called Tzung tzu *(soong soo)*. These are full of meat, nuts and vegetables. Delicious! I liked them a lot.

My grandfather told me that long ago the Dragon Boat Festival was a time for asking the Nature Dragons to help the crops to grow, so there would be plenty of food. Now, though, the festival is a celebration of working and getting on well together.

© Tony Mitton

The Dragon Boat Festival

The Chinese Dragon Boat Festival – Tuan Yang Chieh – is usually held in June. According to the story, a poet fell out with his Emperor and threw himself into a lake and drowned. The people did not want his body to be eaten by fish and demons so they threw rice into the water and made loud noises. Today in China, people have races in decorated boats with dragon heads, and eat rice dumplings wrapped in leaves to celebrate the festival.

Personal, social and emotional development

★ Discuss the dangers of water and remind the children that they must be careful near water. Talk about learning to swim.
★ Using the photocopiable sheet on page 85, cut out two dragon shapes for each child. Encourage them to draw one with a fierce face and one with a calm face.

Communication, language and literacy

★ Look at books about dragons, such as *Dragons and Monsters* by Anita Ganeri (Macdonald Young). Describe the dragons, their colours and the texture of their skin.
★ Give each child a copy of the photocopiable sheet on page 85. Invite them to draw rows of scales using handwriting patterns.

Mathematical development

★ Fill a large tub with uncooked rice and provide a set of balancing scales and measuring cups. Encourage the children to count the cups as they measure onto one of the scales. How many cups will they need on the other side to make them balance? How many cups to fill the scales to the top on both sides? How many cups are left in the tub?

Knowledge and understanding of the world

★ Add a paper clip to a paper boat and try to move the boat with a magnet.
★ Examine cooked and uncooked rice. Include long grain, risotto and Basmati rice.

Physical development

★ Divide the children into two groups. Give one group some drums. Ask the other group to join together, one by one, each holding on to the person's waist in front to make a dragon boat. As they move around, the drummers should try to keep a steady beat.

Creative development

★ Cut the shape of a dragon from a roll of stiff paper. Provide red and green fabric scraps, glue and spreaders. Invite the children to decorate the dragon shape. Display the completed dragon during the festival.
★ Make dragon boats to race in a water tray. Provide margarine tubs and cardboard outlines of dragons' heads and tails. Encourage the children to draw faces and decorate the tails using marker pens, then attach these to the tubs with sticky tape.

Early years wishing well: Festivals

I made a bracelet

(Tune: 'Here We Go Round the Mulberry Bush')

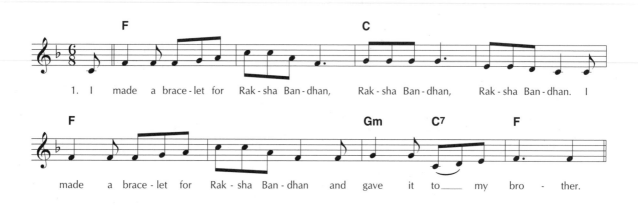

1. I made a brace-let for Rak-sha Ban-dhan, Rak-sha Ban-dhan, Rak-sha Ban-dhan. I made a brace-let for Rak-sha Ban-dhan and gave it to my bro-ther.

2. My brother promised to care for me,
Care for me, care for me.
My brother promised to care for me,
And all on Raksha Bandhan.

© Susan Eames

Early years wishing well: Festivals

I made a bracelet

Raksha Bandhan is a Hindu festival that occurs in August. Sisters give their brothers a bracelet called a rakhi as a sign of protection and to strengthen the bond of love. In return, brothers give their sisters a gift or some money. Sweets and cakes are eaten to celebrate the festival.

Personal, social and emotional development

★ To demonstrate one of the ways that we can care for a family member, invite a parent to bathe or feed a baby for the children to observe. Help the children to list ways that they could help a younger brother or sister.

Communication, language and literacy

★ Show the children how to form letters with a piece of wool or string. Provide card and glue sticks and invite the children to write their name with the glue and then stick on the wool or string.

★ Sing the song 'I made a bracelet' together and then talk about brothers and sisters. Follow up by reading a story about brothers and sisters such as *My Naughty Little Sister* by Dorothy Edwards (Mammoth).

Mathematical development

★ Give the children paper and crayons and ask them to draw a picture of their family. Ask them to count their family members. How many adults are there? How many boys/girls?

★ Let the children sort and count a variety of sequins. Put a good selection in one container and provide several smaller containers for sorting. Decide which sequins would be suitable for decorating a rakhi.

Knowledge and understanding of the world

★ Encourage the children to name body parts. Can they find their wrists? Ankle? Elbow? What do we wear on these parts of our body?

★ Display a collection of bracelets for the children to examine and discuss.

★ Take the children to visit a haberdashers or department store to look at the wide selection of silks and threads available.

Physical development

★ Arrange the children in a circle and sing the song 'I made a bracelet' together, making appropriate actions.

Creative development

★ Let the children weave their own rakhis. Cut strips of plastic netting (vegetable bags are ideal) and provide blunt sewing needles and bright threads. Encourage the children to weave the threads in and out of the netting. Join the ends together with a few stitches.

★ Buy a pack of small fairy cakes from a supermarket and let the children dip these in jam and then roll into desiccated coconut.
NB Check for any nut allergies and dietary requirements.

It's Divali tonight!

Everything's ready to greet the new year.
Everything's bright with light.
Everyone's dressed up and full of joy.
It's Divali tonight.

We've lit the lamps to show the way
Up to our front door.
We've sprinkled coloured powders to make
Patterns on the floor.

We've given each other gifts of sweets.
There's lots of delicious things to eat.

Everything's ready to greet the new year.
Everything's bright with light.
Everyone's dressed up and full of joy.
It's Divali tonight!

© John Foster

It's Divali tonight!

Divali (The Festival of Light) is held in October or November and is celebrated by both Hindus and Sikhs. Hindus celebrate the triumph of good over evil when Rama freed his wife Sita from the demon king, Ravan. They honour Lakshmi, the Goddess of Fortune. There is hand painting called Mendhi, and clay lanterns called divas are burned. People clean their homes, wear new clothes and enjoy fireworks.

Personal, social and emotional development

★ Encourage the children to talk about their own experiences of being good or bad.
★ How do the children feel when they give and receive gifts? Extend the activity by letting the children wrap a few sweets to give as gifts.

Communication, language and literacy

★ Make a Divali card using folded black A4 card. Let the children use a word processor to write a greeting to stick inside. Encourage the children to spread PVA glue on the front of their cards and sprinkle glitter over the glue to resemble the twinkling lights of Divali.

Mathematical development

★ Show the children how to make a rangoli sewing card. Punch holes around the outside of a piece of square card, then thread coloured wool in and out of the holes. More able children can weave patterns using wool in different colours.

★ Take the children on a walk around your local area to look at front doors. Talk about colour, shape and size, and discuss together the features such as numbers, letter boxes and doorknobs.

Knowledge and understanding of the world

★ The Swastika or Shathia is a symbol of good luck and prosperity for Hindus and is a traditional part of the festival. Challenge the children to draw this symbol and display with their artwork. Show the children other symbols of good luck such as horseshoes, black cats, four-leaf clover and pixies.

Physical development

★ Set a trail of 'lamps' for the children to follow. Cut several diva shapes from card and place them on a winding and twisting route for the children to follow.
★ Let the children help to make chapattis. Mix 150–200ml of water with 225g plain wholemeal flour. Knead thoroughly into a dough then divide into six pieces and roll each piece into a ball. Show the children how to flatten the ball and pat it from one hand to the other. Fry the chapattis quickly on either side in an ungreased frying pan.

Creative development

★ Paint simple Mendhi patterns onto the children's hands using a fine paintbrush. Use brown poster paint as this will wash off easily.

Whizz, crackle, bang!

Wait for the evening,
cool and dark.
Wait for the fizzle,
wait for the spark.

Whizz, crackle, bang!
Just watch us go,
golden rain
and sparkling snow.

Whizz, crackle, bang!
in the big, blue night,
making colours
for your delight.

Whizz, crackle, bang!
as we rush up high,
exploding colours
across the sky.

© Tony Mitton

Whizz, crackle, bang!

An important part of the Divali celebrations are the fireworks.

Personal, social and emotional development

★ Chant the poem together. Talk about times when the children have to wait such as snack time or registration. Play 'Pass the Parcel', encouraging the children to share and wait their turn. Ensure that everyone has a turn.

Communication, language and literacy

★ Discuss some of the words used in the poem to describe the sounds of the fireworks. Encourage the children to think of more words. Write them out and display them with the children's artwork.

★ Give each child a piece of paper measuring 14cm by 23cm, and writing and colouring materials. Encourage them to design a firework, and help them to write any words that they wish to include. When the designs are complete, stick them onto kitchen-roll tubes to make free-standing fireworks.

Mathematical development

★ Talk about how high fireworks reach into the sky. Stick a paper line on the wall at child height. Invite the children to use different objects to measure the height of the line. How many bricks high is it? How many boxes high?

★ Roll out a long piece of paper and draw a line from one side to the other. Tell the children that above the line is the sky and below it is the ground. Invite the children to use wax crayons to draw colourful fireworks. When they have finished, count together how many fireworks there are above and below the line. Record this information on the picture, and then display it on the wall.

Knowledge and understanding of the world

★ Collect a number of 'sound' instruments such as saucepans, powdered-milk tins, corrugated plastic or card, bubble wrap and a large spoon. Give the children a small stick and invite them to play with the collection and make loud and quiet sounds.

Physical development

★ Can the children make the loud and quiet sounds of the fireworks as they move? Try stamping, clapping, swishing clothes, pulling Velcro on shoes and so on.

★ Hang a row of foil or card stars at different heights. Invite the children to pretend to be fireworks as they jump up high and try to touch the stars.

Creative development

★ Make a dark den with a large cardboard box, which is big enough for at least two children. Paint the inside black and invite the children to climb in and imagine that they are in a secret place. Provide a torch for those children who are not confident in the dark.

I'm sorry

(based on Yom Kippur – The Day of Atonement)

I'm sorry for the things I've done
I really shouldn't do.
Like shouting and being nasty
I'm sorry if I hurt you.

Please will you forgive me
If I've made you feel so sad?
I promise I will start again
And never be so bad.

I know New Year is coming
I can hear the shofar call.
So I'll really try much harder
To be good to one and all.

© Stevie Ann Wilde

*The shofar is a ram's horn which is blown
to call all Jewish people to say sorry and
ask forgiveness from others ready for the
New Year in September or early October.*

I'm sorry

Nine days after the Jewish New Year (Rosh Hashanah) is Yom Kippur, the Day of Atonement. It is the most important and holy day for Jews and occurs during September or October. People do not work, eat or drink and often spend the day in the synagogue. The shofar, a ram's horn, is blown to signal that it is time to say sorry and ask forgiveness from others. Some wear white as a symbol of purity. Apple and bread dipped in honey is offered to wish everyone a sweet year. Some Jews swing coins secured in a handkerchief over the head as a ceremony to demonstrate the transfer of sin.

Personal, social and emotional development

★ Encourage the children to recall times when they have done things that they should not have. Use a puppet to act out the confessions and invite the children to shout, 'I'm sorry'.

Communication, language and literacy

★ Chant the poem together, then discuss the meaning of some of the words, such as 'sad', 'nasty' and 'hurt'. Finish by discussing words such as 'good', 'promise' and 'forgive'.

Mathematical development

★ Talk about daily routines, focusing on mealtimes. Explain that Jewish people fast from before sunset of Yom Kippur until after sunset the next day. Provide paper plates and play food and calculate how many meals would be missed by inviting the children to set out each meal and then count the total number of meals.
★ Cut an apple into quarters. Discuss how it has changed shape, and count the slices together. Dip the slices into honey and taste them. (**NB** Check for any food allergies and dietary requirements.)

Knowledge and understanding of the world

★ Talk about how the shofar is used. Gather some objects that are used to alert people such as bells, gongs and whistles. Examine and discuss the objects. Which is loudest?

Physical development

★ Give the children a piece of scrunched-up newspaper wrapped in a sock. Make sure that each child has plenty of space and challenge them to swing it above their heads.
★ Invite the children to chant the poem as they march. Ask one child to make the sound of the shofar. When they hear the sound, the others must stand still and be quiet for a moment before they begin to march again.

Creative development

★ Give each child a coiled ram's horn shape which has been cut from card and invite them to decorate their horns. Then make a 3-D display by attaching each horn to a section of cardboard tube before mounting on the wall.

Chinese Moon Festival

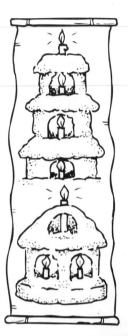

Make sand-castles,
And patterns in the sand.
Put lighted candles in them,
And hold lanterns in your hand.
Now in the darkness,
We'll watch the moon rise,
And picnic on moon cakes,
To find a surprise!

© Jan Pollard

The Moon Festival is held in September, in Hong Kong. People gather on Stanley Beach to have a picnic. The children create castles and patterns in the sand, and fill them with lighted candles. Everyone watches the moon rise and eats moon cakes. These are filled with surprises, for example, dates, coconut, nuts, sesame or lotus seeds.

Early years wishing well: Festivals

Chinese Moon Festival

The Chinese Moon Festival is celebrated in many parts of the Far East in September, when the brightest full moon occurs on the fifteenth day of the eighth lunar month. Special food is prepared, including moon cakes, and lanterns of all shapes, sizes and colours are lit. Offerings of fruit including melons, grapes and peaches are made to the goddess in the moon.

Personal, social and emotional development

★ Ask parents and carers to let their children bring in a piece of fruit to share with the other children. Involve the children in making a fruit salad to share at snack time. (**NB** Check for any food allergies and dietary requirements.)
★ Talk about the children's experiences of seeing the moon. When do we see the moon? Extend the discussion by making the imaginative play area into a bedroom.

Communication, language and literacy

★ Read *Whatever Next!* by Jill Murphy (Macmillan Children's Books) several times. Provide a few props such as a colander, cardboard box and wellington boots, and invite the children to act out the story.

Mathematical development

★ Use the photocopiable sheet on page 92 to demonstrate how the moon changes shape through the month. Copy the sheet onto card and cut out the shapes. Let the children paint them then suspend the shapes in the correct sequence around a hoop.

Knowledge and understanding of the world

★ Talk about the American moon landing on 20 July 1969. Together, look at the book *Moon Landing* (*Discoveries* series, Dorling Kindersley).
★ Carry out an experiment to demonstrate why lanterns are used. Place one candle in a bucket of sand and one inside a garden lantern. Carefully light both candles and take them outdoors. Invite the children to observe them through a window. Which stays alight the longest?

Physical development

★ Develop cutting skills by making lanterns. Fold a piece of coloured A5 paper into a concertina shape. Show the children how to cut shapes from the folded sides, then open the paper out and roll it around a jam jar. Place a tea-light candle inside and observe the light shining through the shapes.

Creative development

★ Give each child a circle of card and encourage them to stick on rice, lentils or wheat grains to make the rocky surface of the moon. When the moons are dry, let the children cover them with foil, gently pressing over the textured surface.

Early years wishing well: Festivals

Toby's apple tree

'Grandad,' said Toby, 'I wish we had a *proper* apple tree in our garden.'

'What's the matter with your apple tree?' asked Grandad.

'The apples aren't very nice,' said Toby. 'They aren't sweet like the ones we buy from the shop.'

'Let's go and have a look at it,' said Grandad, who was looking after Toby for the afternoon.

Toby led the way down to the bottom of the garden, where the apple tree grew. There were several apples in the grass round the tree and Grandad told Toby these were called windfalls, because the wind had blown them down.

'This is a cooking apple tree,' said Grandad. 'We use these apples to make apple pie, or stewed apple.'

'Yuk!' said Toby. '*That* mushy stuff!'

'Why don't you pick me the biggest apple you can find,' said Grandad, 'and bring it along to the kitchen.'

Grandad whistled and Toby watched as Grandad got things out of the kitchen cupboards. He took the big green apple Toby had picked and cut a circle right round it. Then he cut a hole down through the middle, to take out all the pips. Now they were going to fill the hole with good things.

Grandad put the apple in an oven dish.

'Here, you put some sultanas in the hole, Toby,' said Grandad, giving him the packet. Toby pushed the squashy fruits into the hole until it was full.

'Now a spoonful of honey.'

Toby poured a spoon of sticky, golden honey on top of the sultanas.

'And now,' said Grandad, 'some cloves.' He put two little dark brown things into the hole.

'They smell like Christmas!' said Toby.

Grandad put the dish with the apple into the oven.

'We'll wash up now,' he said to Toby, 'and then we'd better go shopping for some ice-cream...'

When they came home, there was a lovely smell in the kitchen. Grandad put on oven gloves and took the dish out of the oven. The apple looked enormous, soft and fluffy. Honey and juice bubbled in the dish.

'This is *baked* apple,' said Grandad. 'We'll let it cool down a bit, and then we'll have it with some ice-cream.'

Toby and his Grandad shared the baked apple. It was delicious.

'This is the yummiest apple in the world,' said Toby. 'I'm glad we've got *our* apple tree!'

© Geraldine Taylor

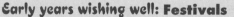

Toby's apple tree

Grandparent's Day is a fairly new celebration, which takes place in September. It is a time for children to appreciate their grandparents and for grandparents to show love for their children's children. Celebrating this special day will help the children to become aware of the strength, information and guidance that older people can offer.

Personal, social and emotional development

★ Ask the children what they think it is like to be a grandparent. Encourage them to think of the positive aspects of being older, such as having more leisure time or time to play with their grandchildren. Do the children's grandparents work or are they retired? Remain sensitive to individual circumstances.
★ Invite the children to bring in photographs of their grandparents to make a wall display.

Communication, language and literacy

★ Compile a questionnaire that the children can take home for a grandparent to complete. For example, 'What are your memories of school?', 'What games did you like to play?'. Discuss the replies and display them.
★ Encourage the children to share any stories that their grandparents have told them.

Mathematical development

★ Make baked apples, just like Toby and his grandad did. Compare different-sized apples, and count and weigh the sultanas.
★ Plant some apple seeds in a shallow tray of wet soil and cover with a plastic bag. Chart and observe their growth

Knowledge and understanding of the world

★ Let the children use their senses to examine spices such as cloves, cinnamon sticks and bark, ground cinnamon and mace.
★ Discuss what the world was like when Grandma and Grandad were young. Set up a display and interest table and ask parents and grandparents to help collect clothes, LP records, toys of their era and other artefacts to bring in to your setting.

Physical development

★ Talk about the importance of keeping fit and active throughout life. Discuss a healthy diet that includes eating fruit such as apples.
★ Dance to the Beatles' song, 'When I'm Sixty Four' from *Sgt Pepper's Lonely Hearts Club Band*'. Include some of the actions.

Creative development

★ Make handprints using bright paint and paper. Mount them and add a caption, then give them to grandparents as a keepsake.
★ Use the photocopiable sheet on page 93 to help the children to make a simple family tree. If this is not appropriate for your children, make up a family tree for the toys in your setting, or for a family from a story-book.

Dancing shoes

(Navaratri story)

Early one morning, Shivani woke up feeling very excited. Today was the beginning of Navaratri, the Hindu festival that led up to Divali – the great Festival of Light. This year it was extra special because Shivani was going to dance the stick dance with her friends for the first time.

After breakfast, the family got ready for the temple. Shivani put on her special dress. It was blue and gold with coloured beads all over it that sparkled and shone.

Mum wore a new red and green sari with gold embroidery around the edge. Dad had new clothes, too.

'Time to go,' said Dad.

'Oh, no!' said Shivani. 'I can't find my shoes. I can't go in bare feet!'

'Shivani, you'll lose your head one day!' said her mum, as she helped her look for them.

They looked in the wardrobe. They looked under the bed. They looked in the cupboard. But they couldn't find Shivani's shoes.

'We're going to be late!' said Dad.

'Here they are!' cried Shivani, waving them in the air. 'They were still in their box!'

They arrived at the temple at last. Pictures and statues of the Hindu goddess had been put up in the middle. Everyone was wearing colourful clothes. They danced and sang to loud, cheerful music.

While the people sang prayers and religious songs, the girls danced around the statue of the goddess. Then it was time for the stick dance.

Shivani ran to her mother. 'I can't find my sticks!' she cried. 'I shall miss the dance!'

Her mother pretended to look for them. 'Oh, Shivani,' she said. 'You'll lose your head one day.' Then she pulled the sticks out from under her chair. 'Here you are,' she smiled.

Shivani laughed and ran to join the other dancers. They banged their sticks together in time to the music to make a loud noise for the celebration. Then they did a clap dance, clapping to the music and dancing round and round.

Shivani twirled round and round in her beautiful new dress that sparkled and shone, until she couldn't dance any more. She went back to sit with her mother and watch the others dancing. She was very tired.

'I do love Navaratri,' she said, sleepily. 'And I'm glad I didn't lose my shoes... or my sticks... or my head!'

© Stevie Ann Wilde

Dancing shoes

Navaratri is marked by a special dance performed by women, in which they sing and clap hands. It is celebrated from the first night of Asvina, in September or October, to honour the Hindu goddess, Durga. Special dishes are eaten as part of the celebrations, but it is also a time for fasting.

Personal, social and emotional development

★ Draw around the children's shoes then add the date to the drawings and display them so that the children can compare the different sizes. Repeat the activity later in the year to see if the children's feet have grown.

Communication, language and literacy

★ Write out a name card for each child and hide them. Talk about losing and finding things, and tell the children that you have lost their name cards. Can they find them?
★ Retell the story to the children using actions and props. Hide the props within reach before you start. Begin with stretching when Shivani woke up. Pretend to look under your chair for the shoes. Produce a shoebox and open it up to reveal a pair of ballet shoes. Follow a similar procedure looking for the sticks and find them close by. Finish off in a tired voice!

Mathematical development

★ Working in small groups, count and compare shoes. How many pairs are there altogether? How many shiny shoes? How many with Velcro fastening? If there are three black pairs, how many pairs are not black?

Knowledge and understanding of the world

★ Invite a member of the community to show the children how to fold a sari. Use the photocopiable sheet on page 94 to encourage the children to follow the simple instructions.
★ Take the children outdoors after it has been raining and let them make footprints. Look at and compare the variety of shapes, sizes and patterns that the different shoes make. Watch as the footprints evaporate.

Physical development

★ Encourage the children to hold hands with another child as they twirl around together. Follow this by organizing the children into small groups, and inviting them to hold hands as they dance round and round.

Creative development

★ Talk about Shivani's special dress. Provide a large outline and let the children make a collage using blue and gold foil paper.
★ Make decorative 'dancing shoes'. Draw around a child's shoe to make a template. Place this onto a carpet offcut and cut two soles. Cut 10cm by 6cm strips of coloured plastic from a carrier bag and let the children decorate them with sequins. Attach the strips to the carpet pieces using PVA glue.

The Harvest Festival

Today is our Harvest Festival. We all have to take some food to playgroup. I have some apples from our tree. My friend Tamara has a tin of beans and a loaf.

We give the food to Mrs Wilson, our playgroup leader, and she puts it on the table. There are lots of different sorts of food: fruit and vegetables, tins and packets. Someone has brought a big, golden pineapple with long, prickly leaves. It looks delicious.

While we play with the toys, Mrs Wilson and the other playgroup teachers put the food into the boxes that we decorated yesterday. I can see my box. I covered it with red and yellow flowered paper. Tamara painted hers with pink and white stripes.

'I wonder who's got the pineapple!' I whisper to Tamara. It's not in my box, or hers.

When all the boxes are full, Mrs Wilson says that we are going to take them to the old people who live on their own or who can't afford to buy very much. Like Mr Archer, who lives on our street. We put on our coats and hats and pick up our boxes of food. Then we set off with Mrs Wilson and the other playgroup ladies.

We stop at lots of different houses. At each house, Mrs Wilson chooses one of us to walk down the path with her and give our box of food to the person who lives there. They are very pleased when they see all their food! I hope I can give my box of food to Mr Archer. I am sure he will like it.

I still haven't seen the pineapple.

Now we are walking along my street. I point out our house to Tamara. Mummy sees us and waves out of the window. I wave back. Then we stop outside Mr Archer's house.

'Come on, Zoe, it's time to deliver your box,' says Mrs Wilson to me.

Smiling, I knock on Mr Archer's door.

'Hello, Mr Archer,' says Mrs Wilson. 'We've brought you some food from our Harvest Festival.'

'What a lovely surprise. Thank you,' says Mr Archer as I give him the box of food. He looks inside and smiles. 'All my favourites!' he says.

That was the last box, so we go back to playgroup. Mrs Wilson says she has a special Harvest Festival surprise for 'all her little helpers': a lovely, juicy ring of fresh pineapple!

© Karen King

Early years wishing well: Festivals

The Harvest Festival

Harvest celebrates the time when the crops are gathered. Harvest suppers are traditional and special hymns are sung at the Church of England's service in October.

Personal, social and emotional development

★ Talk about harvest and where food comes from. Cut pictures of food from magazines and let the children make favourite food collages.
★ Lay a table with a table-cloth, mats, bread basket and place settings for a small group of children. Tell the children that it is for a special harvest supper and join them in their play to reinforce good table manners.

Communication, language and literacy

★ Place some fresh vegetables including carrots, potatoes and turnips in the imaginary play area to extend the children's role-play.
★ Read *Handa's Surprise* by Eileen Browne (Walker Books), using real fruit as props.
★ Give each child some pastry and help them to mould it into the initial of their name. Bake in a moderate oven for about 20 minutes.

Mathematical development

★ Sing and do the actions to 'Five Currant Buns in a Baker's Shop' from *This Little Puffin...* compiled by Elizabeth Matterson (Puffin). Enhance the counting and subtracting by making five buns from clay or salt dough for the children to hold. Paint a

different number of currants on each bun.
★ Provide wholemeal and white bread and a choice of fillings. Cut a slice of bread in half and encourage the children to spread margarine over both halves. Let them spread on the filling and put the two halves together. What shape have they made?

Knowledge and understanding of the world

★ Cut the tops off carrots and parsnips and place them in a shallow tray of water. Let the children observe them for a week or so as the vegetables begin to sprout.
★ Look at books such as *WorldFocus* series (Heinemann) and discuss harvests around the world.

Physical development

★ Help the children to grind some wholewheat grains (available from health food shops) using a pestle and mortar, or the end of a rolling-pin on a board. Show them the flour that they have produced.
★ Give the children a selection of unwashed vegetables to scrub clean. Provide small brushes, water, a tray and paper towels to dry the vegetables.

Creative development

★ Let the children paint boxes to display food for the festival. Provide shoeboxes, poster paints and brushes. When dry, line the boxes with tissue or crêpe paper.

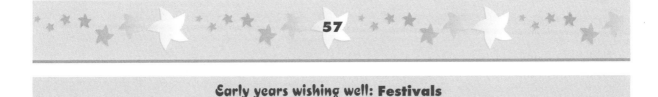

What have you brought?

1. What have you brought for the Har-vest to-day? What have you brought for the Har-vest to-day?

What have you brought for the Har-vest to-day, Please tell us what you've brought.

Chorus I have brought a *— * * Yes that is what I've brought.

Acummulative repeat — *Repeat as needed*

Last time Thank you for all of the things you have brought. Thank you for all of the things you have brought.

Thank you for all of the things you have brought And thank you God as well.

tin of...
bag of...
bunch of...
box of...
pocket of...
bundle of...

*Repeat this bar as many times as necessary so that the song builds up. The response will depend on what has been brought.

© Peter Morrell

Early years wishing well: Festivals

What have you brought?

After a successful harvest, people give thanks for the food that they eat and give food to those who are less fortunate. This can provide an opportunity for children to explore different containers and wrapping used to preserve food.

Personal, social and emotional development

★ Hold a harvest festival and invite parents and carers to let their children bring in items of food to be donated to the needy.

★ To encourage the children to say 'thank you', play a game of 'Snap'. Before anyone picks up the cards they have won, they must say 'thank you'. If they forget, the other player gets the cards!

Communication, language and literacy

★ Look at the words and pictures on a variety of food containers. Can the children recognize any of the words? How do they know what is inside the containers?

★ Collect some items of food and unwrap them. Discuss the food and wrappers and then invite the children to match the wrappers to the food.

Mathematical development

★ Provide a large grocery box for a group activity of junk modelling. Give the children a variety of boxes and encourage them to work together to make one large model.

★ Let the children play with several containers at the water tray. Take two different-shaped bottles containing the same amount. Which one is biggest? Which one holds the most? Let the children fill both bottles using a measuring jug to discover the answer.

Knowledge and understanding of the world

★ Talk about packaging and the important job that it does in preventing food from drying out. Demonstrate this by wrapping one small piece of cheese in cling film and leaving another piece unwrapped. What happens to each piece of cheese?

Physical development

★ Place a large cardboard box, a smaller tin and a stiff paper bag side by side. Stand the children in a line and challenge them to throw a beanbag into each.

★ Sing the song together and then look at the food that has been donated. Act out how it was harvested, for example, reaching up high to pick apples, bending over to pull up carrots, hauling in fishing nets and so on.

Creative development

★ Invite the children to decorate empty margarine tubs by sticking on tissue paper with glue and a spreader, building up layers until the tubs are completely covered. Fill the special boxes with biscuits or cakes for the harvest festival.

Bonfire night

(Tune: 'Old MacDonald Had a Farm')

1. Dress up warm on Bon - fire night, Bon - fire night is great!
Dress up warm on Bon - fire night, We can stay up late. With a
wool - ly scarf and a wool - ly hat, wool - ly scarf, wool - ly hat, wool - ly scarf, wool - ly hat.
Dress up warm on Bon - fire night, Bon - fire night is great!

2. See the fire on Bonfire night,
Bonfire night is great!
See the fire on Bonfire night,
We can stay up late.
With an orange flame and a
    yellow flame,
Orange flame, yellow flame,
Orange flame, yellow flame,
See the fire on Bonfire night,
Bonfire night is great!

3. Hear the sounds on Bonfire night...
With a bang bang bang!
And a whoosh whoosh whoosh!

4. Lovely fire on Bonfire night...
With a sausage roll and a piece
of cake...

> *Let the children sing in two groups, for example (1) 'woolly scarves' (2) 'woolly hats' each time.*

© Ann Bryant

Bonfire night

On 5 November, people light bonfires to commemorate Guy Fawkes' failed attempt to blow up the Houses of Parliament in the Gunpowder Plot of 1605.

Personal, social and emotional development

★ Talk about staying up late. Play a game of 'Sleeping lions'. Tell the children to lie down and pretend to sleep. If they move, they are out and must then watch the others until they are all out.

★ Read 'The firework code' on page 95 several times with the children. Reinforce the danger of fire and the safety rules related to events such as Bonfire night.

Communication, language and literacy

★ Create mini 'bonfires' on individual trays. Put a little wet sand or pebbles in the bottom of the trays, and invite the children to use small twigs and scraps of orange and yellow Cellophane to make flames. Add small figures, trees, fences and gates. Encourage the children to talk about their games.

★ Help the children to compile a list of things that are required for bonfire night, such as warm clothes, hot food, special equipment and so on. Draw and label each item.

Mathematical development

★ Gather together a few sets of gloves and mittens and put one of each pair in a box. Ask the children to choose one of the items from those remaining and challenge them to make a pair.

Knowledge and understanding of the world

★ Set up an interest table on the theme of keeping warm for the children to explore. Include warm clothes, a hot-water bottle, a flask, feathers and sheep's wool.

★ Tell the children that, in the past, people made fires to keep warm. Give the children a small piece of coal to examine, or look at a fireside set together.

Physical development

★ Scrunch up some newspaper and add a few twigs or wooden blocks to make a pretend bonfire. Darken the room and invite the children to hold hands and dance around the bonfire as you sing the song.

★ Let the children rub their hands together vigorously. What happens? Do their hands feel warmer? What other ways can they keep their hands warm?

Creative development

★ Join together several sheets of A3 paper, then encourage the children to work as a group to paint the orange and yellow flames of the bonfire. Provide decorating brushes so that the children can make broad strokes using red and yellow paints. Can they mix the colours to make orange?

Early years wishing well: Festivals

Three kings came riding

Three kings came riding
One, two, three,
Looking for the Baby.
'Where is He?'

Sleeping in a manger
Warm in the hay.
They tiptoed in to see Him
Then they rode away.

© Barbara Garrad

Three kings came riding

On 25 December, the birth of Jesus Christ is celebrated. The three kings travelled from the east, following a bright star, to find the baby Jesus asleep in a manger.

Personal, social and emotional development

★ Talk about how the three kings looked for the baby. How did they find their way? Help the children to memorize the street name where they live. Follow up the activity by finding the different streets on a local map.

Communication, language and literacy

★ Talk with the children about the three kings' journey. What do they think they would have taken with them? Help the children to compile a list, drawing on their own experiences of going on a journey

Mathematical development

★ Lay out sets of three items in the room for the children to find. For example, three chairs together, three books on a table or three boats in the water tray. Can they find the number 3 written anywhere?

★ Give the children various star-shaped items to print with, for example, a pastry cutter, a star cut into a potato, sponge and card stars. Talk about each one. Provide shallow trays containing poster paint and A3 paper, and encourage the children to make several star prints with the different items.

Knowledge and understanding of the world

★ Find out whether hay retains heat. Place one bottle of warm water in a box of hay, and leave another bottle uncovered. Check the bottles later. Has either bottle remained warm? Which is the warmest?

★ Talk about different beds, such as a hammock, a doll's cot and baby's pram. Read *Wake Up, World!* by Beatrice Hollyer (Frances Lincoln) about family life around the world.

Physical development

★ In an open space, encourage the children to gradually raise one hand high into the air and then to open their fingers to make a star shape. Repeat with the other hand. Flutter the fingers to represent twinkling. Finally, keeping arms and fingers outstretched, twirl around the room. Accompany the movement with some gentle music such as 'Caribbean Blue' from *Shepherd Moon* by Enya (Warners).

Creative development

★ Cut out star shapes from card and cut straws into short pieces. Invite the children to stick the straws to the cardboard shapes to make twinkling Christmas stars.

★ Make kings' crowns. Measure around each child's head, then add 3cm and cut out a rectangle to this length and 15cm high. Cut a zigzag along one side. Let the children glue on shiny paper and brightly-coloured foil. Join the ends together with sticky tape.

Santa Claus

(Action rhyme)

Here comes Santa in his sleigh,
high above the town.

(Fly one hand through the air, palm down.)

Look. He's found our chimney.
Now he's climbing down.

(Bring hand to rest against upright other arm, fist closed. This shows sledge parked up against chimney. Show climbing down by using first two fingers walking down upright arm.)

He's picking out our presents
from his big and bulgy sack.

(Mime picking out presents from sack.)

Look. He's found our letter
and our special Christmas snack.

(Look at open palm to show letter. Mime nibbling a mince pie for snack.)

Now he's climbing up again
to get back in his sleigh.

(Show two fingers climbing back up upright forearm. Show sleigh as open hand, palm down, ready to go.)

'Ho, ho, ho!' says Santa
as he hurries on his way.

(Call 'Ho, ho, ho!' from cupped hands. Then show hurrying away with hand as sleigh again, moving through air, palm downwards.)

© Tony Mitton

Santa Claus

There are many different customs and traditions throughout the world to celebrate Christmas. On 24 December, some children hang up stockings for Santa Claus to fill with presents. Santa travels in a sleigh that is pulled by flying reindeer. Santa's sleigh is full of presents and decorated with tinkling bells.

Personal, social and emotional development

★ Develop listening skills by challenging the children to identify different chiming instruments. Can they identify cowbells, a hand bell, a xylophone and a triangle?

★ To help the children to learn the value of giving, invite them to bring a small gift to donate to a children's charity.

Communication, language and literacy

★ Record the children's letters to Santa Claus using a word processor or typewriter. Print the letters for the children to take home and leave out for Santa on Christmas Eve.

★ Read *The Night Before Christmas* by Clement C Moore (OUP). Discuss the children's experiences of Christmas Eve.

Mathematical development

★ Fill a sack with toys and challenge the children to feel from the outside (less able children could feel inside) and guess each item. Include easily recognizable items such as a ball, a ruler and a building block. When the children have identified the items, empty the sack and count how many items altogether. Put one back in the sack. How many are left?

★ Change the words of the counting song 'Ten Green Bottles' to 'Five Red Stockings'.

Knowledge and understanding of the world

★ Take the children for a walk outside. Ask them to look up. What can they see?

★ Using a map of your area, mark out the children's homes where Santa Claus will visit.

Physical development

★ Arrange the children into groups of three and give each group a hoop. Ask one child to be Santa Claus in his sleigh and to stand inside the hoop, and the other two to be reindeer, pulling the hoop along. Play some jingly music such as Prokofiev's 'Troika'.

★ Place hoops on the ground and ask the children to imagine that they are Santa Claus in his sleigh jumping from one roof to another. Can they jump from hoop to hoop?

Creative development

★ Construct sleighs for Santa from a selection of small boxes such as individual cereal boxes. Make a simple template for the sides of the sleigh and invite the children to draw around the template twice on a sheet of thin card, before cutting out the shapes and sticking one to either side of their box. Decorate with sequins and bright collage materials.

New Year promises

This year I promise I'll be good.
I promise I'll do the things I should.

I'll pick my toys up off the floor.
I won't get cross and slam the door.

I won't get up early or stay up late.
I'll always shut the garden gate.

I'll eat my greens. I won't complain.
I'll never ever sulk again.

New Year promises are easy to make.
New Year promises are hard not to break.

© John Foster

Early years wishing well: Festivals

New Year promises

New Year's Day is on 1 January. It is a time when many people resolve to improve on their past behaviour, or set new targets for the future. People count down the seconds to midnight when the old year finishes and the new one begins.

Personal, social and emotional development

★ To make tidying up more enjoyable and to encourage the children to pick toys up off the floor, put on a glove puppet and challenge them to a race, saying, for example, 'Hurry, Mr Fox will put the last brick away'. Try playing a piece of fast music, such as Rimsky-Korsakov's *Flight of the Bumblebee*, and tell the children that everything must be away when the music finishes.

Communication, language and literacy

★ Go on a hunt to find printed dates. Look for examples on newspapers, receipts, letters, envelopes and 'sell by' dates on food.
★ In small groups, ask the children to recall something that has happened to them in the past. Can they remember their birthdays? Talk about future events such as holidays.

Mathematical development

★ Help the children to begin to understand how time is measured by making a photographic record of a child's day. Give the camera to the children's parents and carers to capture the things that happen first thing in the morning and at the end of the day. Display the photographs, noting the times.
★ Compile a chart showing the days of the week on which the children were born. Which is the most popular? How many children were born on the same day?

Knowledge and understanding of the world

★ Display a variety of calendars and diaries. Look at them with the children, pointing out the days of the week. Make a note of the children's birthdays and events that are relevant to them.
★ Tell the children about the custom of waiting for the clock to strike 12 o'clock midnight at the end of the old year and investigate a chiming clock.

Physical development

★ Join hands in a circle, with arms crossed, and sing 'Auld Lang Syne'.

Creative development

★ Let the children draw self portraits on sheets of A4 paper. Glue to A4 card and attach small calendar books (available from newsagents).
★ Paint a paper plate to make a clock-face. Give each child a set of numbers from 1 to 12 and a pair of hands cut from card. Help them to glue the numbers in the correct order. Attach the hands with a split-pin fastener.

Early years wishing well: Festivals

The big steel band

There's a carnival
down the street,
and we clap hands
and stamp our feet
to the sunshine sound of the big steel band.

The floats pass by
all through the day,
and costumed people
swing and sway
to the sunshine sound of the big steel band.

There's a dragon
and there's a king!
We wave and laugh
and cheer and sing
to the sunshine sound of the big steel band.

© Wes Magee

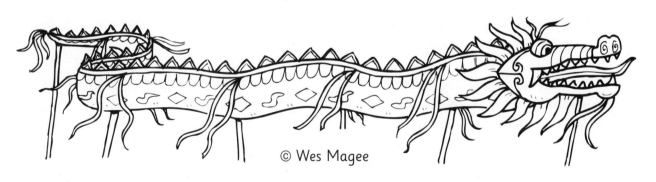

Early years wishing well: Festivals

The big steel band

Carnivals and street parades take place in cities and towns throughout the world and are a time for people to enjoy themselves, wear vibrantly-coloured costumes and play music. Street parades often have elaborate floats.

Personal, social and emotional development

★ Explain to the children that when it is winter in this country, it is summer in other parts of the world and carnivals take place.
★ Invite the children to have their faces painted for the carnival. Use non-toxic face paints and gain parental permission. Keep the designs simple with the emphasis on colour. Let the children see their own painted face in a mirror. Do they look different?

Communication, language and literacy

★ Read stories about carnivals, such as *Nini at Carnival* by Errol Lloyd (Red Fox) and *Spot at the Carnival* by Eric Hill (Frederick Warne).
★ Make imaginary floats. Look at pictures in books for inspiration. Trail crêpe paper and colourful fabrics over chairs. Invite the children to sit on the chairs, and provide drums and shakers for them to play. Encourage plenty of talking, cheering and singing!

Mathematical development

★ Make paper chains from strips of paper measuring approximately 15cm by 3cm. Let the children make repeating colour patterns.

Knowledge and understanding of the world

★ Try making sounds on a variety of steel objects, for example, an upturned saucepan, a saucepan lid or a metal dustbin. Use different beaters such as wooden spoons, metal spoons, beaters covered in cloth or hands only. Talk about the different sounds.

Physical development

★ Play some carnival music that includes a steel drum band. Encourage the children to clap their hands and stamp their feet as they parade around an open space. Can they swing and sway?
★ Help the children to make wands to wave at the parade. Give each child a piece of A4 coloured paper and show them how to roll it into a tube. Secure the tube with sticky tape and cut one end into a frill about 5cm deep.

Creative development

★ Use the template on the photocopiable sheet on page 96 to make masks from stiff paper. Pre-cut the eyeholes, then let the children paint their masks. When dry, glue on coloured feathers or crêpe paper, then attach a lolly stick as a handle. Wear the masks for your own colourful carnival parade.
★ Cut coloured strips of plastic (carrier bags are ideal) measuring approximately 5cm by 10cm and punch a hole in the centre of each. Let the children thread the strips onto lengths of wool to make colourful garlands.

Early years wishing well: **Festivals**

Just a bit of fun

(St Valentine's Day)

Alfie Fox was very surprised when he went for his morning walk through the wood and saw Kate and Marty Squirrel sticking pink paper hearts on all the tree trunks.

'Hello, Alfie,' called Kate. 'We're getting ready for the Valentine's Party tonight. Are you coming?'

'No, I'm not! I don't believe in all that soppy nonsense,' sniffed Alfie.

'It's only a bit of fun,' said Marty, but Alfie had already disappeared down the path.

A little further on, Alfie saw Billy and Jenny Vole blowing up huge, pink, heart-shaped balloons and hanging them from the trees with pink ribbons.

'We're decorating the trees for our Valentine's Party tonight,' said Billy. 'Are you coming, Alfie?'

'No, I'm not! I don't believe in all that soppy nonsense,' sniffed Alfie.

'It's only a bit of fun,' said Jenny, but Alfie had already walked away.

A little further on, Alfie saw Sally and Rick Badger icing a big, heart-shaped pink cake.

'That looks good,' he said, licking his lips. Alfie liked cake.

'It's for our Valentine's Party tonight,' said Sally. 'Are you coming?'

'Oh. No, I'm not!' said Alfie. 'I don't believe in all that soppy nonsense.'

'It's only a bit of fun,' said Rick. But Alfie wasn't listening. He was thinking about that lovely pink cake as he walked away.

When he got home, Alfie was surprised to see a big, pink envelope lying on the mat. Alfie opened it up. Inside was a large card with a big, pink heart shape on the front. *Be my Valentine!* it said. Then, inside, *See You At The Party Tonight.*

'What a lot of soppy nonsense,' said Alfie. But really he was pleased. He'd never had a Valentine's card before.

'I wonder who sent it,' he thought. 'I suppose I'll have to go to the party and find out.'

That evening, Alfie brushed his tail until it was soft and bushy, put on his best waistcoat and set off for the party, with the Valentine's card tucked under his arm.

All the other animals cheered when Alfie arrived.

'I knew you'd come when you saw our card,' smiled Rick.

'So *you* sent me the Valentine's card?' said Alfie, surprised.

'We *all* sent it,' said Jenny, 'because we wanted you to come to the party! We didn't want you to miss all the fun.'

Alfie was pleased to think that the other animals had wanted him to come to the party so much they'd sent him a card.

'Well, I don't believe in all that soppy nonsense,' smiled Alfie. 'But I'm all for a bit of fun!'

And it's good to have friends who care so much about me, he thought to himself as he and Jenny danced together.

© Karen King

Just a bit of fun

Saint Valentine's Day is on 14 February. On this day, friends and lovers exchange cards and presents. There are several versions of the St Valentine story. One is that Saint Valentine was a priest who was killed because he sheltered Christians from the Romans. Another belief is that this is the day on which birds begin to choose their partners and build their nests. Valentine cards were introduced in Victorian times.

Personal, social and emotional development

★ In a small group, ask the children to talk about a special friend. Encourage them to say a few things that they like about them.
★ Talk about how Alfie got ready for the party. Talk about the children's own hair care routine. Who washes and brushes their hair? Provide the children with hairbrushes and combs and let them play with the dolls, preparing them for a party.

Communication, language and literacy

★ Look at a party invitation. Can the children suggest what information they think should be included in an invitation? Help them to write their own invitations.
★ Encourage the children to write the name of a friend across a heart shape cut from coloured paper. Ensure that every child has a named heart and display them on Saint Valentine's Day.

Mathematical development

★ Cut out a set of hearts in various sizes and ask the children to put them in order of size. Ask, 'Which is biggest?', 'Which is smallest?', 'Is this one bigger than that one?'. Take one away and ask how many are left.

Knowledge and understanding of the world

★ Give the children some icing sugar mixed with water and a cocktail stick which has been dipped in red colouring. Observe the icing changing colour as the colouring drips off the cocktail stick. Use the pink icing to spread on plain biscuits.

Physical development

★ Give the children a branch which has at least three prongs. Show them how to weave pink wool in and out of the branches.
★ Tell the children that a ring is a symbol of love. Invite them to hold hands and move around an open space in a ring.

Creative development

★ Make a friendship poster. Print pink handprints and cut them out when dry. Cut a large heart shape from card and stick on the handprints. Add 'We all join hands in friendship' to the middle of the heart.
★ To create a Victorian lace effect, paint one side of a doily and then turn it over and press down to make a print on card. When dry, fold in half to make a Valentine's card.

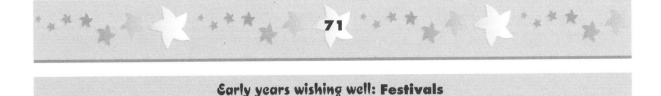

Early years wishing well: Festivals

The pancake race

One cold morning, Luke's mum came into his bedroom.

'It's Shrove Tuesday,' she said as she gave him a hug.

'What's *Shrove* Tuesday?' asked Luke.

Luke knew what *Tuesday* was. It was the day after Monday. It was the day that his teacher always took his nursery class into the big school hall. But this week he had a holiday from school.

'It's a special day when we eat pancakes,' said Mum. 'Pancake Day. We're going into the village this morning to watch the pancake race.'

'What's a pancake race?' asked Luke.

'You'll see,' said Mum, with a laugh.

Luke wanted so much to know what the pancake race was that he quickly got dressed and ate his breakfast. Then he cleaned his teeth, pulled on his wellingtons and fetched his coat and scarf and woolly hat from the hall.

'Ready!' he said, smiling at Mum.

There were a lot of people hurrying past the house. Luke and his mum joined them.

'Come on,' said Mum. 'Let's find the best place to stand.'

They stood in a crowd of people near a rope that stretched right across the road.

'Is this where the race finishes?' asked Luke.

His mum nodded.

In the distance, Luke could see a row of people standing in the middle of the road.

'They'll get run over,' he said, but his mum shook her head.

'Not today,' she said. 'The road has been closed for the race.'

Suddenly, there was a loud shout.

'READY, STEADY, GO!' Everyone in the row began to run towards Luke. They were carrying frying pans and tossing pancakes in the air as they ran. They looked very funny. Luke began to laugh as people around him started to shout.

Some people dropped their pancakes, but they picked them up and ran on, tossing the pancakes high in the air. They came nearer and nearer and the shouting crowd grew louder and louder. Luke jumped up and down with excitement.

'Come on!' he shouted.

A young woman flashed past Luke and ran through the rope.

'Hooray!' shouted the crowd. 'The winner!'

'Hooray!' shouted Luke. It had been very exciting, but it was over very quickly.

'We'll have pancakes for tea,' said Mum when they were on their way home.

'Not the same ones they were tossing in the race, I hope!' laughed Luke.

© Jill Atkins

Early years wishing well: Festivals

The pancake race

Shrove Tuesday is the day before Lent, and takes place during February or March. Pancakes were cooked to use up all the eggs and fat in the house in preparation for fasting during Lent.

Personal, social and emotional development

★ Practise tossing a pancake. Give the children a plastic frying pan and a small pancake. Let them toss the pancake up in the air and try to catch it!
★ Talk about hygiene in the kitchen, stressing the importance of washing hands, keeping surfaces clean and discarding any food that has been dropped on the floor.

Communication, language and literacy

★ Read and discuss the story *The Big Pancake* (*Favourite Tales* series, Ladybird).
★ Set up a pancake restaurant in the role-play area and help the children to compile a menu with a variety of different pancake fillings and toppings.

Mathematical development

★ Investigate shapes by printing with different objects such as corks, sponges and wooden blocks. Give the children some paper and a tray of poster paint, and encourage them to examine each shape before they make a print. Can they compare the flat shape in the picture to the 3-D shape?

★ Lay a circular cloth on the floor. How many children can stand around it? How many can sit on it? How many can lay on it? Fold the cloth in half and ask what shape it is. Fold it in half again to demonstrate another shape.

Knowledge and understanding of the world

★ Provide some pancake toppings to taste. Include lemon, sugar, honey, margarine and jam. Discuss the different flavours. Which are the children's favourites? (**NB** Check for any food allergies and dietary requirements.)

Physical development

★ Cut a pancake shape from thick paper and draw on an arrow. Stand the children in a line, side by side, and give the first child a plastic frying pan. Encourage them to toss the 'pancake' and move one step in the direction that the arrow is pointing. Continue until the children have all moved in many directions.
★ Lemon juice is a traditional topping for pancakes. Let the children use a citrus press to squeeze fresh lemons.

Creative development

★ Lay a large sheet of paper on the floor (outdoors is best for this messy activity). Give the children round sponges and trays containing different-coloured poster paints. Let them dip the sponges in the paint and then drop them onto the paper to make colourful prints.

Early years wishing well: **Festivals**

A letter to a pen pal

(Chinese New Year)

To my dear friend, Richard,

Today I saw a Lion, dancing in my street! He was brightly coloured with red and gold streamers. He had a huge mouth with flashing white teeth. He had large black eyes that stared at me. He also had a long winding body that swished this way and that. Can you imagine this? Really it was two men dressed up in a lion costume and they did the Lion Dance in the big procession through our town. There were firecrackers and drums and clashing cymbals making a terrible noise. Of course it's our Chinese New Year Festival! It can be anywhere between 21 January and 20 February.

Did you know that every year is named after an animal? These are the twelve animals. The Rat, Ox, Tiger, Rabbit, Dragon, Snake, Horse, Ram, Monkey, Chicken, Dog and Pig.

We are having a super time with lots of celebrations. My mum cleaned the house yesterday with a brush to sweep out any bad things that happened last year.

We have a statue of a special god of the house. He is supposed to tell the chief god, the Jade Emperor, if we have been well behaved this year. So we try to be very good and kind to people.

My dad bought lots of fruit and flowers to have in our house to bring us good luck and a long life.

The street processions are very exciting and everyone goes outside to watch. Maybe next Chinese New Year you can come to our house to visit and enjoy a very Happy New Year.

With love and greetings from your friend, Li Chan.

© Stevie Ann Wilde

Early years wishing well: Festivals

A letter to a pen pal

Chinese New Year is one of the most important festivals for Chinese communities around the world and occurs during late January or February. Each year is named after an animal. Ang Pows (lucky bags) containing money are given and many homes have a flowering bush for good luck.

Personal, social and emotional development

★ Talk about how each Chinese year got its name. Make a chart to show which Chinese year each of the children were born in. Include your own birth year and those of other staff members.

Communication, language and literacy

★ Help the children to write a letter. Give them paper and marker pens and ask them to draw a picture of one of their recent activities. Encourage more able children to write a few words. Help them to sign their name and then let them give the letters to friends or relatives.
★ Write out the greeting 'Kung Hei Fat Choi', which means 'Happy New Year'. Give the children tracing paper and pencils and ask them to trace over it.

Mathematical development

★ Invite the children to make Ang Pows using red paper into rectangles measuring approximately 21cm by 8cm. Ask them to shape one end into a curve, then fold up to the curve. Use a glue stick to glue each side. Talk about the shape and how it has changed. Put a few chocolate coins into each Ang Pow.

Knowledge and understanding of the world

★ Cook noodles for a snack and let the children observe them before and after cooking. (**NB** Check for any food allergies and dietary requirements.)
★ Brew a variety of China teas such as Peking, Lapsang Souchong and Yunnan. When the teas are cool, let the children taste, smell and discuss them. (**NB** Check for any food allergies and dietary requirements.)

Physical development

★ Invite half of the group to wear masks (see below) for a lion dance, encouraging them to swish this way and that. Give the remainder of the group drums and cymbals to accompany the dancing.

Creative development

★ Let the children make lion masks. Provide circles cut from stiff paper and encourage the children to paint them and add facial features. Attach strips of crêpe paper around the face as a mane. Thread wool or elastic either side of the mask and tie around the child's head.
★ Invite the children to paint cardboard tubes in red and gold paint to make a firecracker decoration. When dry, string them together and hang up during the celebrations.

Early years wishing well: Festivals

Eid-ul-Fitr

My name is Mariam. My family is Muslim and today we are going to the mosque. We are going to celebrate the end of Ramadan which has been a time of fasting. My mum and dad did not eat anything between sunrise and sunset for a whole month. My brother, Fozia, and I didn't fast because we are too young. Now the fast is over and we are celebrating the Eid-ul-Fitr festival.

I am wearing my new clothes to go to the mosque. It is called my shalwar-kameez. Fozia is wearing his new kurta-pyjamas.

This morning we all gave gifts to each other. My parents are also giving money to poor people so that they can enjoy the festival as well. All the adults stayed awake to watch the new moon rise to show it was the end of Ramadan and the beginning of Eid.

I've made a pretty card to give to my parents and one for Fozia as well. I've written Eid Mubarak in Urdu. This means Happy Eid.

After we've been to the mosque we are having a big feast with rice and vegetables and curried lamb. I can hardly wait for that!

Tomorrow, at school, we are having a big party to celebrate. We will all wear our new clothes and a photographer is coming to take a picture of our class! Mum's calling me to go to the mosque now. Bye bye and Eid Mubarak!

© Stevie Ann Wilde

Eid-ul-Fitr

Eid-ul-Fitr falls at the end of Ramadan when Muslims fast for 30 days from dawn to dusk. There are special prayers, gifts for the poor and readings of the Koran during this period. The fast ends on the morning after the sighting of the new moon, and the first food to be eaten is a date. People wear new clothes and exchange cards.

Personal, social and emotional development

★ Encourage the children to consider those less fortunate than themselves. Ask parents and carers to let their children bring in a few pennies to donate to a local charity. As the children arrive, ask them to lay out the pennies in a line. Decide together who to donate the money to.

Communication, language and literacy

★ Discuss the meaning of the word breakfast – to break a fast. What do the children like to eat in the mornings?

★ Make Eid posters. Write out 'Eid Mubarak. Happy Eid' using a highlighter pen and invite the children to write the greeting using the highlighter marks as a guide.

Mathematical development

★ Ask the children to suggest food that they would like to include in a feast. Write out a shopping list, encouraging the children to state quantities and sizes of each item. Include prices and let more able children use a calculator to add up how much the feast will cost.

Knowledge and understanding of the world

★ Soak half a packet of dried dates in water overnight. Let the children examine and taste the dried and the soaked dates. Compare taste, colour and texture. (**NB** Check for any food allergies and dietary requirements.)

Physical development

★ Talk about sunrise and sunset. Ask the children to curl up small, then uncurl slowly, pretending that they are the sun rising. Tell them to stretch up their arms and stand on tiptoe to represent the full sun. Reverse the action as the sun sets. Extend the activity with a similar routine to make a moonlit sky.

Creative development

★ Show the children how to cook rice and vegetables to eat at snack time. (**NB** Check for any food allergies and dietary requirements.) Wash the rice in a sieve before cooking. Let the children look at the contents of a packet of frozen vegetables before cooking. Mix the cooked ingredients together.

★ Invite the children to make Eid cards. Tell them that Muslims write from right to left and that their cards open the opposite way to the cards that we normally make and send. Decorate with self-adhesive stars and moons and write 'Eid Mubarak' inside the cards.

Early years wishing well: Festivals

Who will be in Bethlehem?

(Tune: 'I Saw Three Ships')

1. Now who will be in Beth-le-hem, In Beth-le-hem, in Beth-le-hem? Now who will be in Beth-le-hem on Christ-mas day in the morn-ing?

2. There's Mary and there's Joseph, too
In Bethlehem, in Bethlehem.
There's Mary and there's Joseph, too
On Christmas Day in the morning.

3. The ox and ass and sheep are there
In Bethlehem, in Bethlehem...

4. The shepherds walk down from the hills
To Bethlehem, to Bethlehem...

5. The angels tell us Christ is born
In Bethlehem, in Bethlehem...

6. The three kings travel from the east
To Bethlehem, to Bethlehem...

7. And Jesus Christ was born for us
In Bethlehem, in Bethlehem...

© Peter Morrell

Who will be in Bethlehem?

Christmas Day, on 25 December, is when Christians celebrate the birth of Jesus Christ. He was born in a stable in Bethlehem, surrounded by animals. Angels, shepherds and three kings visited Him, bringing a message of peace on Earth.

Personal, social and emotional development

★ Think about the word 'peace'. Do the children know what it means? Talk about the animals sharing the stable and the three kings bringing gifts. Remind the children of the times that they have been kind and unselfish.

★ Sing *Silent Night* in a hushed voice. Talk about times when it is necessary to be quiet, such as when a baby is sleeping.

Communication, language and literacy

★ Sing the song together and then discuss the people and animals mentioned. Ask the children to role-play the Christmas story, letting them choose their characters.

★ Read some nativity stories, such as *Jesus' Christmas Party* by Nicholas Allen (Red Fox) and *The Story of Christmas* by Anita Ganeri (Dorling Kindersley). Compare the pictures and look for similar words in each book.

Mathematical development

★ Using the animals and figures, let the children play out the words of the song. Ask, 'How many people are there in the stable?',

'How many animals?', 'Who travelled the furthest to Bethlehem?'.

Knowledge and understanding of the world

★ Tell the children about north, east, south and west. Use a compass to show them which direction is east.

★ Talk about the birth of Jesus and how he grew up to be an adult. Extend the discussion by displaying photographs of people at different stages of life.

★ Look at an atlas or globe to show the children where Bethlehem is in relation to where they live.

Physical development

★ Act out the song as you sing. Begin quietly in the stable, then walk down from the hills, outstretched arms as angels, then be the three kings travelling as if on camels. Finish by curling up small as Jesus in a manger.

★ Let the children wrap up a doll in a sheet, encouraging them to hold the baby carefully. Can they carry it safely and smoothly across the room?

Creative development

★ Invite the children to make observational paintings of the animals in the song. Set out a few plastic animals, paper, water paints and brushes. Encourage the children to mix the colours to match that of the animal that they have chosen to copy.

March of the candles

Intro

1. March of the can-dles one two three, Which night of Ha-nuk-kah? Let's see?

If it's the first night we'll light one And hap-py we will be.
second two
third three
fourth four

Play 4 times

March of the can-dles one two three, Which night of Ha-nuk-kah? Let's see?

If it's the fifth night we'll light five And hap-py we will be.
sixth six
seventh seven
eighth eight

Play 4 times

© Johanne Levy

March of the candles

Hanukkah, the Feast of Lights or Feast of Dedications, commemorates the day on which the Jewish people won their right for religious freedom. The holiday, usually held in December, is celebrated by lighting eight candles in a candlestick called a menorah.

Personal, social and emotional development

★ Look at coloured and fragranced candles. Which ones are the children's favourites?
★ Discuss other special occasions when candles are used, for example, on birthday cakes or during Advent.

Communication, language and literacy

★ Write on a sheet of white paper with a white candle. Paint over the entire sheet to reveal the words.
★ Smooth over a piece of clay and make eight holes in which to place candles. Invite the children to use a skewer to write out the letters of Hanukkah in the clay.

Mathematical development

★ Hanukkah lasts for eight days. Have a number eight day, involving counting and sorting. For example, find eight shells hidden in sand or thread eight buttons onto string.
★ Count the correct number of candles for Hanukkah and note the sequence for lighting. On the first day, light one candle, on the second day, two and so on, until the eighth

day when all eight candles are lit. Candles are added from right to left but are burned from left to right. The newest candle is lit first.

Knowledge and understanding of the world

★ Place different-sized candles in a safe place and light them. Let the children see what happens when they burn.
★ Discuss how candles were once the main form of lighting in the home.

Physical development

★ Children receive a present every night during the festival. Ask each child to select eight empty cardboard boxes and try wrapping them using paper and sticky tape.
★ Encourage the children to sing the song as they march around the room holding up a finger for each candle.

Creative development

★ Invite the children to make menorah cards. Fold a rectangular piece of card in half lengthways and attach eight card candle shapes across the top.
★ Show the children a picture of the Star of David. Provide them with paint and sponges cut into equal-sided triangles. Can they sponge-print a similar star?
★ Focus on blue and white for a painting activity, explaining to the children that these are the colours of the Israeli flag and figure prominently during Hanukkah.

Early years wishing well: Festivals

Happy Holi

Hopping frog

Welsh cakes

To make 16 Welsh cakes

200g plain flour

1 level tsp baking powder

a pinch of salt

50g butter or margarine

50g solid vegetable fat

50g caster sugar

50g currants

1 egg (beaten)

2 tbsps milk (approximate)

caster sugar to dredge

1 Sift the flour with the baking powder and salt.

2 Rub in the fats; add the sugar and currants.

3 Add the egg and sufficient milk to make a stiff paste.

4 Roll out to 1cm thick and cut into rounds using a 7cm cutter.

5 Grease a griddle or heavy frying pan and heat gradually each side until golden brown.

6 Sprinkle with sugar and cool on a wire rack.

7 Serve alone or with butter.

Saint George and the dragon

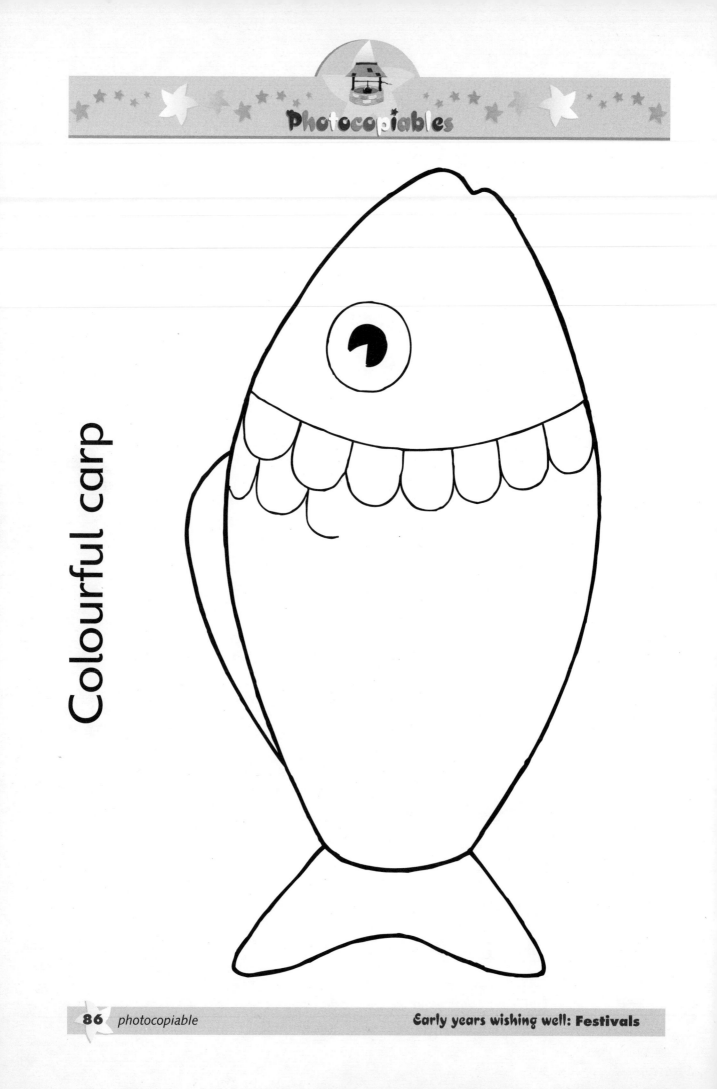

Colourful carp

Easter tree

Flower parts

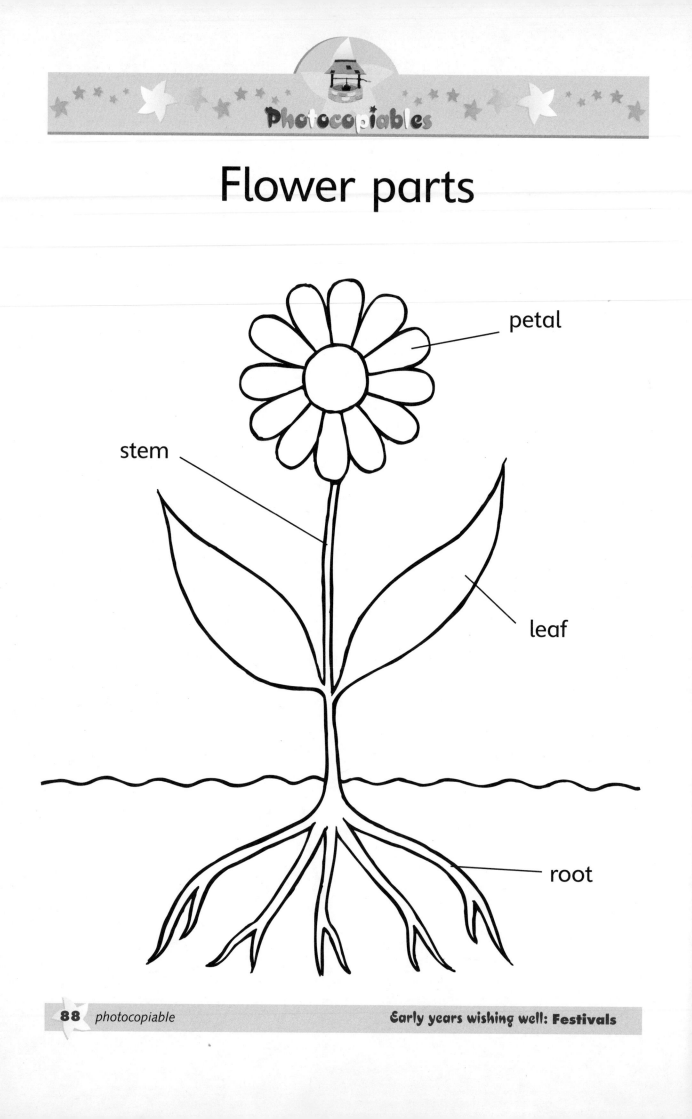

petal

stem

leaf

root

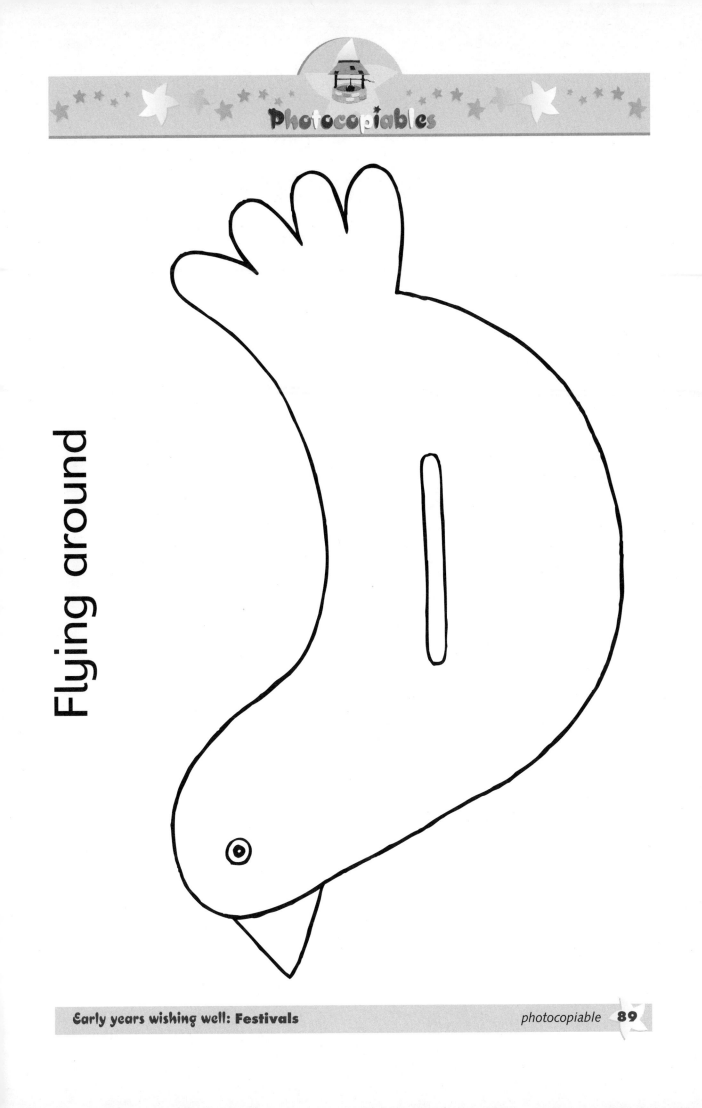

Flying around

Spotty tie

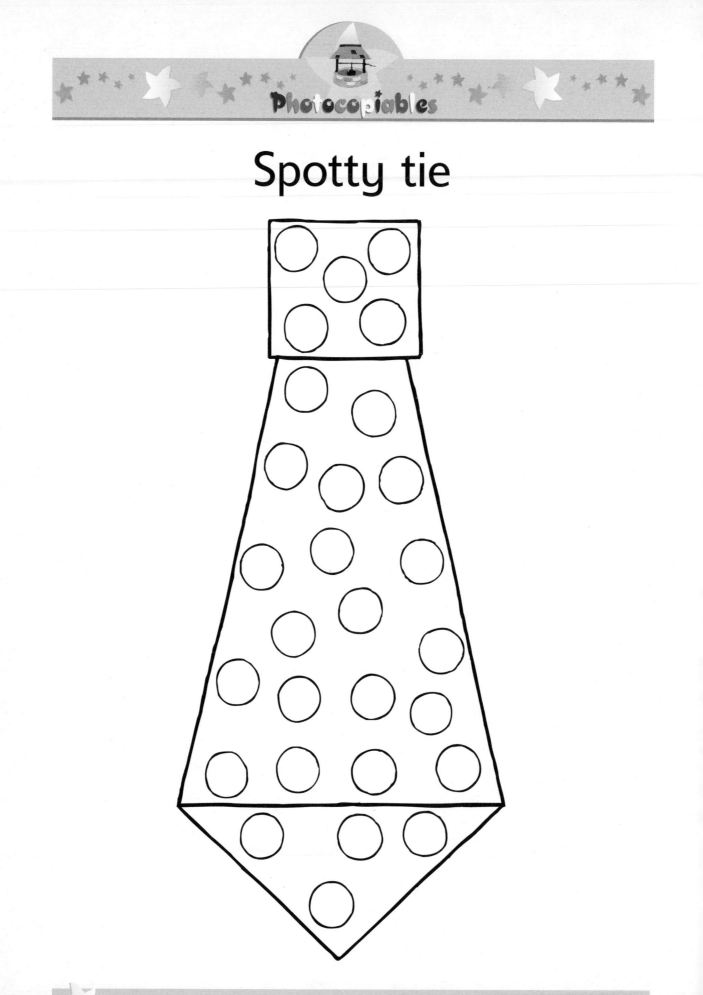

Linking elephants

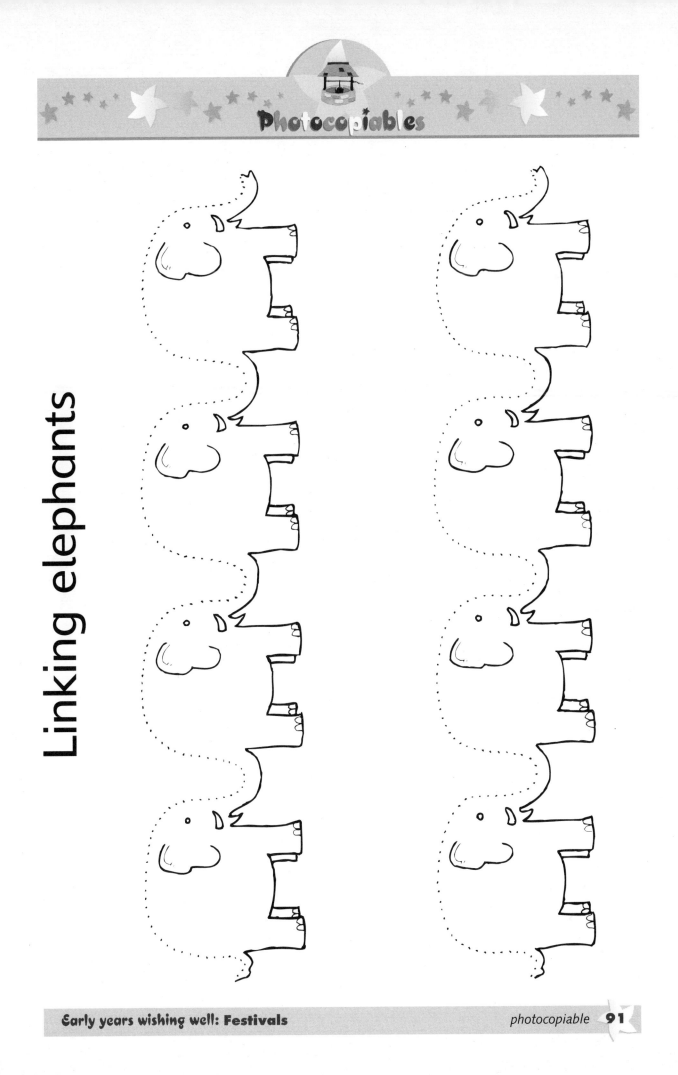

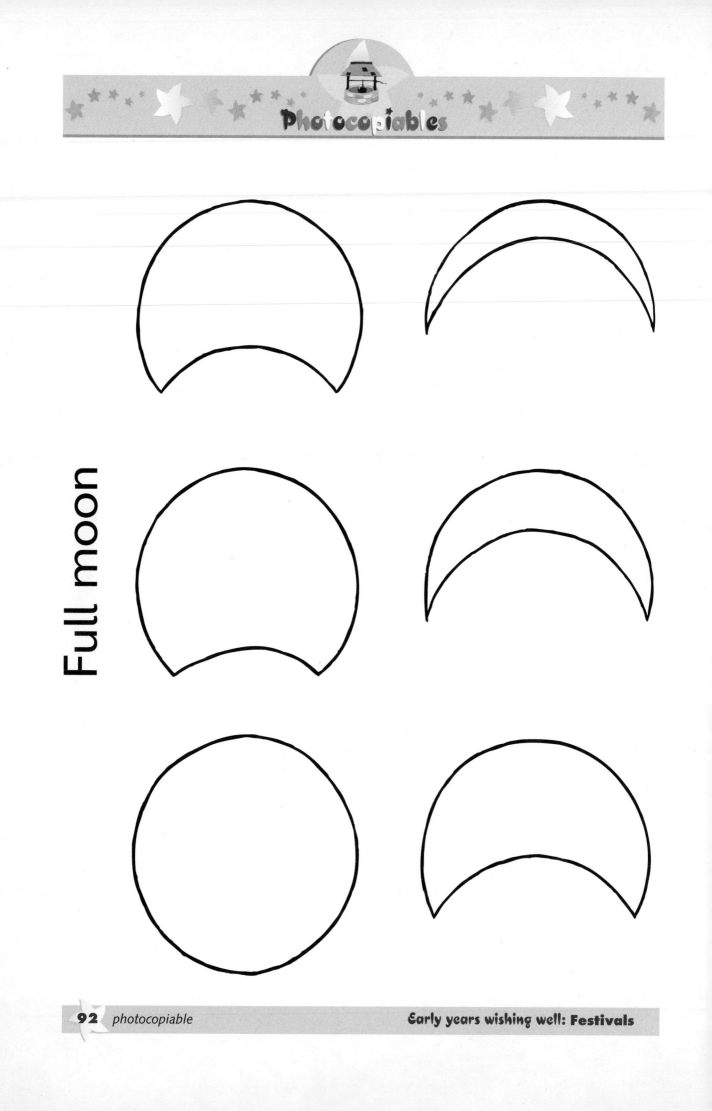

Full moon

Family tree

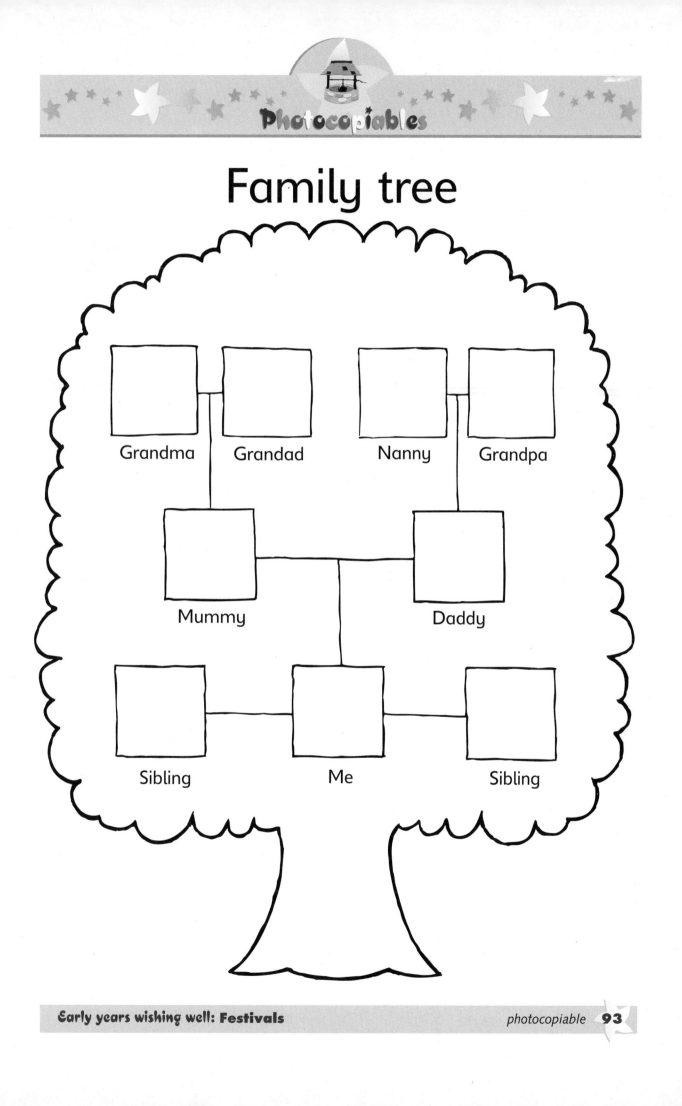

Dressing up: How to put on a sari

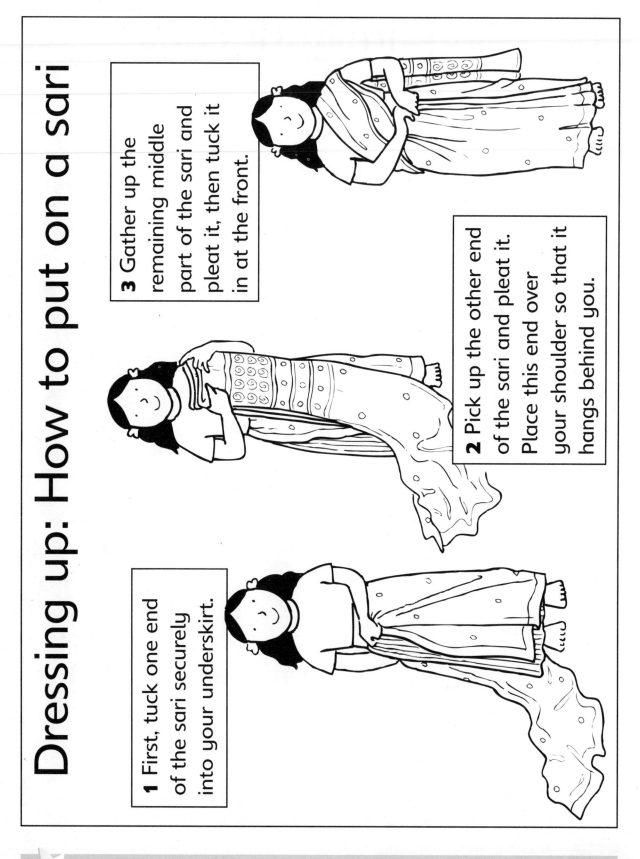

3 Gather up the remaining middle part of the sari and pleat it, then tuck it in at the front.

2 Pick up the other end of the sari and pleat it. Place this end over your shoulder so that it hangs behind you.

1 First, tuck one end of the sari securely into your underskirt.

The firework code

1 Keep fireworks in a closed box; take them out one at a time and put the lid back on at once.

2 Follow the instructions on each firework carefully; read them by torchlight, never by a naked flame.

3 Light fireworks at arm's length – preferably with a safety lighter or fuse wick.

4 Stand well back.

5 Never return to a firework once lit – it may go off in your face.

6 Never put fireworks in your pocket.

7 Keep pets indoors.

8 Never fool with fireworks.

Carnival mask